Sock Art
Bold, Graphic Knits for Your Feet

First published in Great Britain 2013 by
Search Press Limited, Wellwood, North Farm Road, Tunbridge Wells, Kent TN2 3DR

Also published in the United States of America in 2013 by
Trafalgar Square Books, North Pomfret, Vermont 05053

Originlly published in German as *Sockenkunst im Jacquard-Look*

© 2010 frechverlag GmbH, 70499 Stuttgart, Germany (www.frechverlag.de)
English translation © 2013 Trafalgar Square Books

The instructions and materials lists in this book were carefully reviewed by the authors and the staff of the publisher. However, accuracy cannot be guaranteed. The authors and publisher cannot be held liable for errors.

This edition is published by arrangement with Claudia Böhme Rights & Literary Agency, Hannover, Germany (www.agency-boehme.com).

ISBN: 978-1-84448-940-4

Library of Congress Control Number: 2012950745

PROJECT MANAGEMENT: Eva Barbara Hentschel
TECHNICAL EDITOR: Edeltraut Söll
LAYOUT: Petra Theilfarth
PHOTOS: frechverlag GmbH, 70499 Stuttgart; lighting, Michael Rudder, Stuttgart
TRANSLATION FROM GERMAN: Donna Druchunas
ENGLISH TECHNICAL EDITOR: Carol Huebscher Rhoades

Printed in China

10 9 8 7 6 5 4 3 2 1

WE WOULD LIKE TO THANK COATS GMBH (KENZINGTON), LANA GROSSA (GAIMERSHEIM) AND SCHOELLER SÜSSEN GMBH (SÜSSEN) FOR THEIR SUPPORT IN THE CREATION OF THIS BOOK.

Edelgard Janssen • Ute Eismann

Sock Art

Bold, Graphic Knits for Your Feet

Search Press

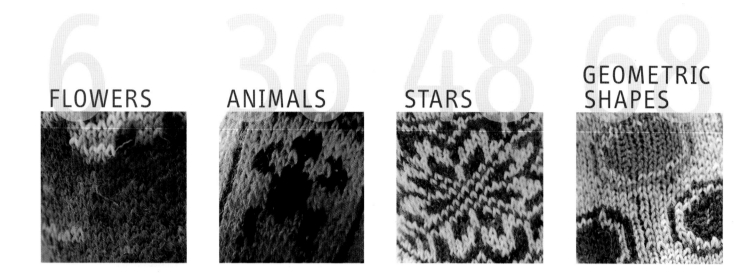

It is impossible to know exactly when the technique of jacquard or two-color stranded knitting originated. One thing is certain: it owes its name to the French mechanic and silk-weaver Joseph Marie Jacquard who invented the Jacquard loom over 200 years ago. It was the first loom to automate the process of weaving "jacquard" or brocade printed fabrics.

Knitting similar designs— colorful motifs on a plain background—is relatively simple. The patterns are usually represented by charts that accurately reflect the design. When working small pattern repeats, the unused yarn is stranded loosely across the back of the knitting. Jacquard patterns basically consist of one main background color and one or more contrasting pattern colors.

The 1950s were a high point in the history of two-color knitting. Stranded knitting designs appeared in winter fashion collections around the world. Whether on the ice, hiking, skiing or in the ski lodge, jacquard-knitted sweaters, hats, scarves and gloves were not only very chic but quite indispensable.

Today, jacquard knitting has become classic, and the variety of patterns and colors are limitless. Sock knitting seems to be especially suited to experimenting with color patterns. Socks knit up quickly, and let you easily try out new patterns and colors combined into imaginative designs. With just a little practice and imagination, you can create wonderful little works of wearable art!

The inspirations for the socks in this book are as varied as the patterns themselves: They come from travel, nature, and art. We invite you to dive in with us into the world of two-color stranded sock knitting, and even to experiment with creating your own designs. Knit and enjoy!

Flowers

Violets, petunias, and tulips bring color to your sock drawer while daffo-dils, tulips, and forget-me-nots conjure up spring in the dead of winter. For a summer mood, decorate your socks with bellflowers and colorful bouquets. Bright and bold, subtle hues or delicate shades — it's color that makes these socks cause a stir.

COLORFUL
FLOWER GARDEN
Instructions page 20

**DELICATE
VIOLETS**
Instructions page 22

TULIPS AND ORNAMENTS

Instructions page 32

HIDDEN FORGET-ME-NOTS

Instructions page 34

Chart 1

Chart 2

TULIPS IN BERRY COLORS

Instructions page 18

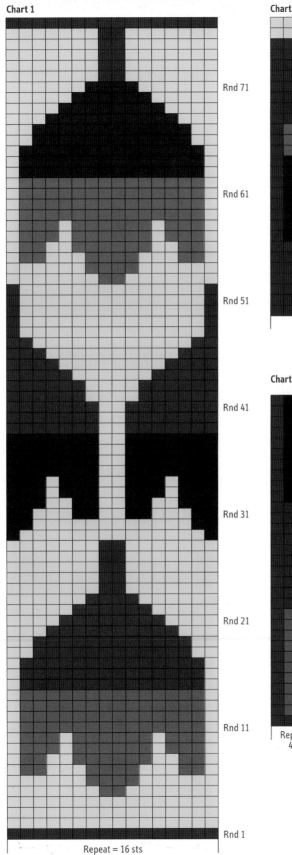

Rnd 71

Rnd 61

Rnd 51

Rnd 41

Rnd 31

Rnd 21

Rnd 11

Rnd 1

Repeat = 16 sts

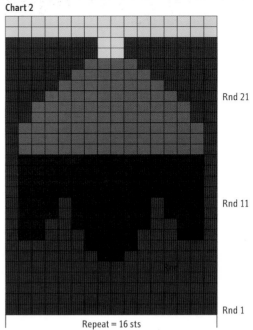

Rnd 21

Rnd 11

Rnd 1

Repeat = 16 sts

Chart 3

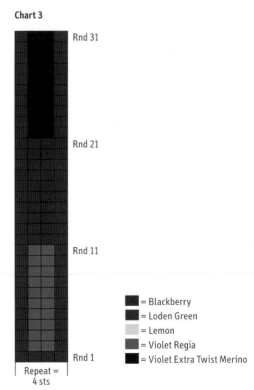

Rnd 31

Rnd 21

Rnd 11

Rnd 1

Repeat = 4 sts

■ = Blackberry
■ = Loden Green
□ = Lemon
■ = Violet Regia
■ = Violet Extra Twist Merino

Tulips in Berry Colors

LEVEL OF DIFFICULTY
Experienced

SIZE
Women's small

MATERIALS
Yarn:

Fingering (CYCA #1)

Regia 4-ply (75% wool/
25% nylon; 229 yd / 210
m/50 g), Loden Green
(#1994), Lemon (#2019),
40 g each, and Violet
(#2020), approx 20 g

Regia Extra Twist Merino
(75% Merino wool/25%
nylon; 229 yd / 210 m/50 g),
Violet (#9354), approx 20 g

Austermann Step Classic
(75% wool/25% nylon;
460 yd / 421 m/100 g),
Blackberry (#1021),
approx 20 g

Needles: Set of 5 dpn U.S.
size 0 (2 mm) or size needed
to obtain gauge.

GAUGE
29 sts and 37½ rnds =
4 x 4 in (10 x 10 cm) over
Chart 1

35½ sts and 38½ rnds =
4 x 4 in (10 x 10 cm) over
Chart 3

PATTERN STITCHES

STOCKINETTE STITCH (ST ST)
Working back and forth: knit RS rows, purl WS rows.
In the round: knit all rounds.

REVERSE STOCKINETTE STITCH (REV ST ST)
In the round: purl all rounds.

GARTER STITCH
Working back and forth: knit every row.

CHART NOTES
Charts 1 and 2 are worked in St st in the round. Each square
represents one stitch and each row in the chart represents
one round or row of knitting. When changing colors, strand
the unused yarn loosely on the back of the work, making
sure the tension remains even. To avoid long floats, twist
the working yarns around each other after every 2 to 3
stitches. Chart 1 has a repeat of 16 sts worked over 77
rounds and Chart 3 has a repeat of 4 sts worked over 31
rounds. Chart 2 is worked back and forth for 28 rows over
the 16 heel stitches.

INSTRUCTIONS

With Loden Green, CO 64 sts. Divide sts evenly on 4 dpns
and join to work in the round, being careful not to twist
cast-on row.

CUFF
Work 18 rnds (approx 1¼ in / 3.5 cm) in St st and then purl
2 rnds.

LEG
Begin working Chart 1, working 4 repeats of 16 sts around.
The end of the rnd is between needles 1 and 4. Work all 77
rnds of Chart 1 (approx 8 in / 20.5 cm).

DUTCH HEEL (SEE PAGE 92)
With Loden, work the heel back and forth over the 32 sts on
needles 1 and 4 as follows:
Work the first and last 4 sts of each row in garter st, and the
middle 24 sts in St st. Work Chart 2 over the center 16 sts of
the heel until all rows of chart are complete (approx 2¼ in /
6 cm).

TURNING THE HEEL
With Lemon, follow basic instructions for turning a Dutch
heel, working until decreases are made with the 2 sts
before and after the center 10 sts—12 sts rem in heel.

INSTEP SHAPING
Continuing with Lemon, return to knitting in the round,
picking up and knitting 14 sts along each side of the heel
flap plus 1 extra st on each side between the heel and the
instep sts. Needles 2 and 3 have 16 sts each, and needles 1
and 4 now have 21 sts each—74 sts total. The end of the rnd
is between needles 1 and 4.
Next rnd: Knit around.
Dec rnd: Knit to last 3 sts on ndl 1, k2tog, k1; knit across
needles 2 and 3; on ndl 4, k1, ssk, knit to end of rnd.
Repeat dec rnd every 3rd rnd 4 times—64 sts rem.

FOOT
Work in St st with Lemon until 15 rnds have been worked
and foot measures approx 1¼ in / 3.5 cm), then work all 31
rnds of Chart 3 (approx 3¼ in / 8 cm).

TOE

With Loden, work in St st.

Rnd 1: Knit.

Dec rnd: *Knit to last 3 sts on ndl 1, k2tog, k1; on ndl 2, k1, ssk, knit to end of needle; rep from * again on needles 3 and 4.

Repeat dec rnd every 4th rnd twice, and then every other rnd 9 times—12 sts rem.

FINISHING

Break the yarn and run the tail through the remaining sts. Pull gently to fasten off. Weave in ends neatly on WS.

Make a second sock the same way.

Colorful Flower Garden

SIZE
Women's small

MATERIALS
Yarn:

Fingering (CYCA #1)

Austermann Step Classic
(75% wool/25% nylon;
460 yd / 421 m/100 g),
Pink (# 1016), 30 g

Austermann Royal (60%
Merino wool/20%
nylon/10% cashmere/10%
silk; 219 yd / 200 m/50 g),
Dark Pink (# 21), 20 g

Schoeller + Stahl Fortissima
(75% wool/25% nylon;
229 yd / 209 m/50 g),
Fuchsia (# 405) and Grass
Green (#1006), 20 g each

Regia 4-ply (75% wool/
25% nylon; 229 yd / 210
m/50 g), Charcoal heather
(#522), 30 g

Needles: Set of 5 dpn U.S.
size 0 (2 mm) or size needed
to obtain gauge.

GAUGE
30½ sts and 34½ rnds =
4 x 4 in (10 x 10 cm) over
Chart 1

33½ sts and 41½ rnds =
4 x 4 in (10 x 10 cm) over
Chart 2

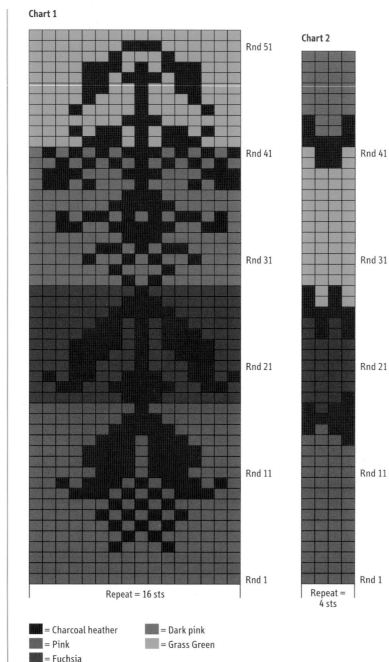

Chart 1

Rnd 51

Rnd 41

Rnd 31

Rnd 21

Rnd 11

Rnd 1

Repeat = 16 sts

Chart 2

Rnd 41

Rnd 31

Rnd 21

Rnd 11

Rnd 1

Repeat =
4 sts

■ = Charcoal heather   ■ = Dark pink
■ = Pink   ■ = Grass Green
■ = Fuchsia

PATTERN STITCHES

RIBBING
All rnds: (K2, p2) around.

STOCKINETTE STITCH (ST ST)
Working back and forth, knit RS rows,
purl WS rows.
In the round, knit all rounds.

GARTER STITCH
Working back and forth, knit every
row.

CHART NOTES
Charts 1 and 2 are worked in St st in
the round. Each square represents
one stitch and each row in the chart
represents one round or row of knitting. When changing colors, strand
the unused yarn loosely on the back
of the work, making sure the tension
remains even. To avoid long floats,
twist the working yarns around each
other after every 2 to 3 stitches. Chart
1 has a repeat of 16 sts worked over
52 rounds and Chart 2 has a repeat of
4 sts worked over 50 rounds.

INSTRUCTIONS

With Charcoal heather, CO 64 sts.
Divide sts evenly on 4 dpns and join to
work in the round, being careful not
to twist sts.

CUFF

Work 21 rnds (approx 2¼ in / 5.5 cm) in Ribbing as follows: *With Pink knit 2, with Charcoal heather purl 2; rep from * to end of rnd, stranding unused color in back of work.

LEG

Begin working Chart 1, working 4 repeats of 16 sts around. The end of the rnd is between needles 1 and 4. Work all 52 rnds (approx 6 in / 15 cm).

DUTCH HEEL (SEE PAGE 92)

With Charcoal heather, work the heel back and forth over the 32 sts on needles 1 and 4 as follows: Work the first and last 3 sts of each row in garter st, and the middle 26 sts in St st. Work back and forth in patt as est for 24 rows (approx 1¾ in / 4.5 cm).

TURNING THE HEEL

With Charcoal heather, follow basic instructions for turning a Dutch heel, working until decreases are made with the 2 sts before and after the center 12 sts—14 sts rem in heel.

INSTEP SHAPING

With Pink, return to knitting in the round, picking up and knitting 12 sts along each side of the heel flap plus 1 extra st on each side between the heel and the instep sts. Needles 2 and 3 have 16 sts each, and needles 1 and 4 now have 20 sts each—72 sts total. The end of the rnd is between needles 1 and 4.

Begin following Chart 1 and, *at the same time*, dec as follows:

Next 3 rnds: Knit around.

Dec rnd: Knit to last 3 sts on ndl 1, k2tog, k1; knit across needles 2 and 3; on ndl 4, k1, ssk, knit to end of rnd.

Repeat dec rnd every 3rd rnd 3 times—64 sts rem.

FOOT

Continue working Chart 2 until all 50 rnds have been worked (approx 4¾ in / 12 cm).

TOE

With Charcoal heather work in St st.

Rnd 1: Knit.

Dec rnd: *Knit to last 3 sts on ndl 1, k2tog, k1; on ndl 2, k1, ssk, knit to end of needle; rep from * on needles 3 and 4.

Repeat dec rnd every other rnd 5 times, then every rnd 7 times—12 sts rem.

FINISHING

Break the yarn and run the tail through the remaining sts. Pull gently to fasten off. Weave in ends neatly on WS.

Make a second sock the same way.

Delicate Violets

LEVEL OF DIFFICULTY
Intermediate

SIZE
Women's medium/men's small

MATERIALS
Yarn:

Fingering (CYCA #1)

Regia 4-ply (75% wool/ 25% nylon; 229 yd / 210 m/ 50 g), White (# 600), 40 g, Fir (#327), 20 g, Fern (#1092), and Black (#2066), 10 g each

Lana Grossa Meilenweit 50 (80% wool/20% nylon; 229 yd / 210 m/50 g), Violet (#1336), 20 g

Schoeller + Stahl Fortissima 100 (75% wool/25% nylon; 460 yd / 421 m/100g), Purple (#2095), 20 g

Needles: Set of 5 dpn U.S. size 1-2 (2.5 mm) or size needed to obtain gauge.

GAUGE
28½ sts and 40½ rnds = 4 x 4 in (10 x 10 cm) over Chart 1

32 sts and 36½ rnds = 4 x 4 in (10 x 10 cm) over Chart 2

PATTERN STITCHES

RIBBING
All rnds: (K2, p2) around.

STOCKINETTE STITCH (ST ST)
Working back and forth, knit RS rows, purl WS rows. In the round, knit all rounds.

GARTER STITCH
Working back and forth, knit every row.

CHART NOTES
Charts 1 and 2 are worked in St st in the round. Each square represents one stitch and each row in the chart represents one round or row of knitting. When changing colors, strand the unused yarn loosely on the back of the work, making sure the tension remains even. To avoid long floats, twist the working yarns around each other after every 2 to 3 stitches. Chart 1 has a repeat of 17 sts worked over 69 rounds and Chart 2 has a repeat of 16 sts worked over 53 rounds.

INSTRUCTIONS

With White, CO 64 sts. Divide sts evenly on 4 dpns and join to work in the round, being careful not to twist sts.

CUFF
Work 25 rnds (approx 2 in / 5 cm) in Ribbing.

LEG
Begin working Chart 1, working 4 repeats of 17 sts around. The end of the rnd is between needles 1 and 4. Work all 69 rnds of Chart 1 (approx 6¾ in / 17 cm).

DUTCH HEEL (SEE PAGE 92)
With Fir, work the heel back and forth over the 34 sts on needles 1 and 4 as follows:
Work the first and last 4 sts of each row in garter st, and the middle 26 sts in St st. Work in patt as est until 26 rows have been completed (approx 2 in / 5 cm).

TURNING THE HEEL
With Fir, follow basic instructions for turning a Dutch heel, working until decreases are made with the 2 sts before and after the center 10 sts—12 sts rem in heel.

INSTEP SHAPING
Continuing with Fir, return to knitting in the round, picking up and knitting 13 sts along each side of the heel flap plus 1

extra st on each side between the heel and the instep sts. Needles 2 and 3 have 17 sts each, and needles 1 and 4 now have 20 sts each—74 sts total. The end of the rnd is between needles 1 and 4. Begin working Chart 2 and, *at the same time,* dec as follows:

Next rnd: Knit around.

Dec rnd: Knit to last 3 sts on ndl 1, k2tog, k1; knit across needles 2 and 3; on ndl 4, k1, ssk, knit to end of rnd.

Repeat dec rnd every 3rd rnd 2 times then every other rnd 2 times—64 sts rem.

FOOT

Work even until all 53 rows of Chart 2 have been worked (approx 5¾ in / 14.5 cm).

TOE

With White, work in St st.

Rnd 1: Knit.

Dec rnd: *Knit to last 3 sts on ndl 1, k2tog, k1; on ndl 2, k1, ssk, knit to end of needle; rep from * on needles 3 and 4.

Repeat dec rnd every other rnd 3 times, then every rnd 10 times—8 sts rem.

FINISHING

Break the yarn and run the tail through the remaining sts. Pull gently to fasten off. Weave in ends neatly on WS.

Make a second sock the same way.

Chart 1

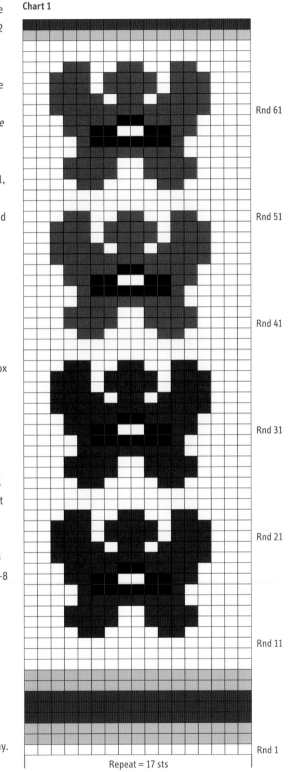

Rnd 61

Rnd 51

Rnd 41

Rnd 31

Rnd 21

Rnd 11

Rnd 1

Repeat = 17 sts

Chart 2

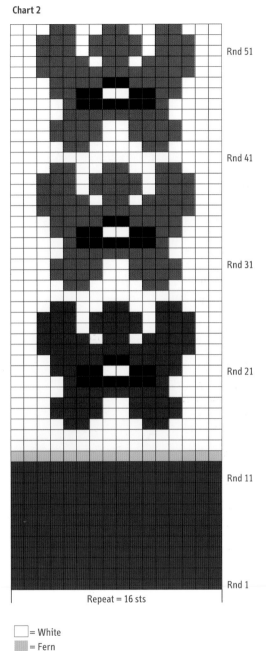

Rnd 51

Rnd 41

Rnd 31

Rnd 21

Rnd 11

Rnd 1

Repeat = 16 sts

☐ = White
▨ = Fern
▨ = Fir
▨ = Purple
▨ = Violet
■ = Black

Purple Flowers with Polka Dots

LEVEL OF DIFFICULTY
Intermediate

SIZE
Women's medium/men's small

MATERIALS
Yarn:

Fingering (CYCA #1)

Lana Grossa Meilenweit Merino (80% Merino wool/20% nylon; 460 yd / 421 m/100g), Violet (#2005), 50 g and May Green (#2018), 10 g

Lana Grossa Meilenweit 50 (80% wool/20% nylon; 230 yd / 210 m/50 g), Mauve (#1343) and Plum (#1340), 10 g each

Regia 4-ply (75% wool/ 25% nylon; 229 yd / 210 m/ 50 g), Violet (#2020), 10 g

Schoeller + Stahl Fortissima (75% wool/25% nylon; 229 yd / 209 m/50 g), Violet (#1014), 10 g

Needles: Set of 5 dpn U.S. size 0 (2 mm) or size needed to obtain gauge.

GAUGE
32 sts and 38½ rnds = 4 x 4 in (10 x 10 cm) in Flower Pattern

32 sts and 40½ rnds = 4 x 4 in (10 x 10 cm) in Polka Dot Pattern

Chart

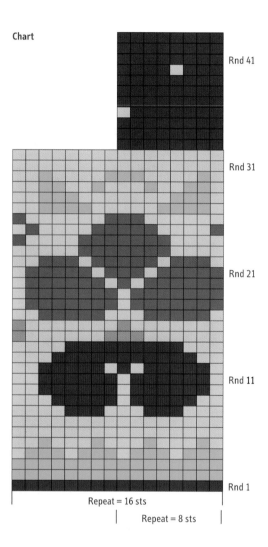

Rnd 41

Rnd 31

Rnd 21

Rnd 11

Rnd 1

Repeat = 16 sts

Repeat = 8 sts

■ = Violet Meilenweit Merino
■ = May Green
■ = Mauve
■ = Plum
■ = Violet Regia
■ = Violet Fortissima

PATTERN STITCHES

RIBBING
All rnds: (K2, p2) around.

STOCKINETTE STITCH (ST ST)
Working back and forth, knit RS rows, purl WS rows.
In the round, knit all rounds.

GARTER STITCH
Working back and forth, knit every row.

CHART NOTES
The charted pattern is worked in St st in the round. Each square represents one stitch and each row in the chart represents one round or row of knitting. When changing colors, strand the unused yarn loosely on the back of the work, making sure the tension remains even. To avoid long floats, twist the working yarns around each other after every 2 to 3 stitches. The Floral Pattern has a repeat of 16 sts and 32 rounds and the Polka Dot Pattern has a repeat of 8 sts and 8 rounds. For the sock, chart rows 1-32 are worked once, then rows 36-43 are repeated for the Polka Dot pattern.

INSTRUCTIONS

With Meilenweit Merino in Violet, CO 64 sts. Divide sts evenly on 4 dpns and join to work in the round, being careful not to twist sts.

CUFF
Work 24 rnds (approx 2¼ in / 5.5 cm) in Ribbing.

LEG

Begin working charted pattern, working 4 repeats of 16 sts around for Floral Pattern and 8 repeats of 8 sts around for Polka Dot Pattern. The end of the rnd is between needles 1 and 4. Work all rnds of Floral Pattern then 22 rnds of Polka Dot Pattern (approx 5½ in / 14 cm).

DUTCH HEEL (SEE PAGE 92)

With Mauve, work the heel back and forth over the 32 sts on needles 1 and 4 as follows:
Work the first and last 3 sts of each row in garter st, and the middle 26 sts in St st. Work in patt as est until 28 rows have been completed (approx 2¼ in / 5.5 cm).

TURNING THE HEEL

With Mauve, follow basic instructions for turning a Dutch heel, working until decreases are made with the 2 sts before and after the center 12 sts—14 sts rem in heel.

INSTEP SHAPING

With Meilenweit Merino in Violet, return to knitting in the round, picking up and knitting 14 sts along each side of the heel flap plus 1 extra st on each side between the heel and the instep sts. Needles 2 and 3 have 16 sts each, and needles 1 and 4 now have 22 sts each—76 sts total. The end of the rnd is between needles 1 and 4.
Resume working Polka Dot Pattern as charted and, *at the same time*, dec as follows:
Knit 2 rnds even.
Dec rnd: Knit to last 3 sts on ndl 1, k2tog, k1; knit across needles 2 and 3; on ndl 4, k1, ssk, knit to end of rnd.
Repeat dec rnd every 3rd rnd 5 times—64 sts rem.

Note To maintain the Polka Dot Pattern while decreasing, in the 3rd round at the end of needle 1 and at the beginning of needle 4, work 9 sts in Violet between the Mauve sts.

FOOT

Work in St st in Polka Dot Pattern for 65 rnds (approx 6¼ in / 16 cm).

TOE

With Mauve work in St st.
Rnd 1: Knit.
Dec rnd: *Knit to last 3 sts on ndl 1, k2tog, k1; on ndl 2, k1, ssk, knit to end of needle; rep from * on needles 3 and 4.
Repeat dec rnd every other rnd 5 times, then every rnd 7 times—12 sts rem.

FINISHING

Break the yarn and run the tail through the remaining sts. Pull gently to fasten off. Weave in ends neatly on WS.

Make a second sock the same way.

Magnificent Petunias

LEVEL OF DIFFICULTY
Easy

SIZE
Women's medium/men's
small

MATERIALS
Yarn:

Fingering (CYCA #1)

Regia 4-ply Color Classics
Denim Black (#1933), 30 g
and Flusi Fraulein (#1804),
20 g

Regia 4-ply (75%
wool/25% nylon; 229 yd /
210 m/50 g), Violet (#2020),
10 g

Regia Extra Twist Merino
(75% wool/25% nylon;
229 yd / 210 m/50 g), Violet
(#9354), 20 g

Schoeller + Stahl Fortissima
(75% wool/25% nylon;
229 yd / 209 m/50 g),
Fuchsia (#1012), 20 g

Needles: Set of 5 dpn U.S.
size 0 (2 mm) or size needed
to obtain gauge.

GAUGE
29 sts and 36 rnds = 4 x 4 in
(10 x 10 cm) over Charted
Pattern

Chart

Rnd 51

Rnd 41

Rnd 31

Rnd 21

Rnd 11

Rnd 1

Repeat = 16 sts

PATTERN STITCHES

RIBBING
All rnds: (K2, p2) around.

STOCKINETTE STITCH (ST ST)
Working back and forth, knit RS rows, purl WS rows.
In the round, knit all rounds.

CHART NOTES
The charted pattern is worked in St st in the round. Each
square represents one stitch and each row in the chart represents one round or row of knitting. When changing colors,
strand the unused yarn loosely on the back of the work,
making sure the tension remains even. To avoid long floats,
twist the working yarns around each other after every 2 to 3
stitches. The Flower Pattern has a repeat of 16 sts worked
over 54 rnds.

INSTRUCTIONS

With Denim Black, CO 64 sts. Divide sts evenly on 4 dpns
and join to work in the round, being careful not to twist sts.

CUFF
Work 21 rnds (approx 2 in / 5 cm) in St st.

= Denim Black
= Violet Regia 4-ply
= Flusi Fraulein
= Violet Extra Twist Merino
= Fuchsia

LEG

Begin working Floral Pattern, working 4 repeats of 16 sts around. The end of the rnd is between needles 1 and 4. Work all 54 rnds of chart (approx 6 in / 15 cm).

SHORT-ROW HEEL (SEE PAGES 90-91)

With Fuchsia, work the heel back and forth in St st over the 32 sts on needles 1 and 4 as follows (see pages 90-91 for basic short-row heel technique):

Divide the heel stitches into 3 sections with 10 sts in the center and 11 sts on each side. Work decreasing short-row section, using the double-stitch technique for working turns. When 10 sts rem in center, work the next 2 rows to the end of the heel sts, picking up the double loops and knitting them together, then work to the beginning of the center section. Work increasing short-row section, using the double-stitch technique and completing heel as described in the basic instructions.

FOOT

Return to working in the round, picking up the double loops and knitting them together on first rnd—64 sts.

Work rows 14-54 of Floral Pattern chart, aligning repeats with those on the leg (approx 4½ in / 11.5 cm).

TOE

With Denim Black, knit 2 rnds. Change to Fuchsia.

Rnd 1: Knit.

Dec rnd: *Knit to last 3 sts on ndl 1, k2tog, k1; on ndl 2, k1, ssk, knit to end of needle; rep from * on needles 3 and 4.

Repeat dec rnd every 3rd rnd 4 times, then every rnd 9 times—8 sts rem.

FINISHING

Break the yarn and run the tail through the remaining sts. Pull gently to fasten off. Weave in ends neatly on WS.

Make a second sock the same way.

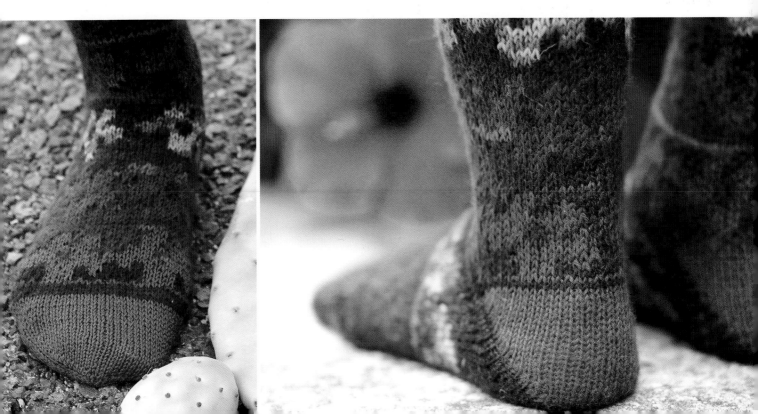

Pastel Daffodils

LEVEL OF DIFFICULTY
Intermediate

SIZE
Women's medium/men's small

MATERIALS
Yarn:

Fingering (CYCA #1)

Regia 4-ply (75% wool/ 25% nylon; 229 yd / 210 m/ 50 g), Gray-blue Heather (#1980), 30 g, Super White (#2080), Ice Blue (# 2018) and Fern (#1092), 20 g each

Needles: Set of 5 dpn U.S. size 0 (2 mm) or size needed to obtain gauge.

GAUGE
29 sts and 33 rnds = 4 x 4 in (10 x 10 cm) over Chart 1

30½ sts and 36 rnds = 4 x 4 in (10 x 10 cm) over Chart 2

Chart 2

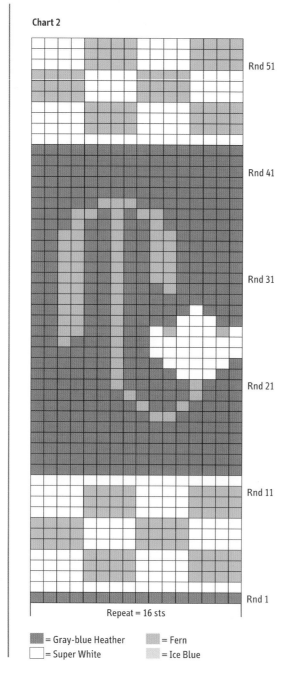

Rnd 51
Rnd 41
Rnd 31
Rnd 21
Rnd 11
Rnd 1

Repeat = 16 sts

Chart 2

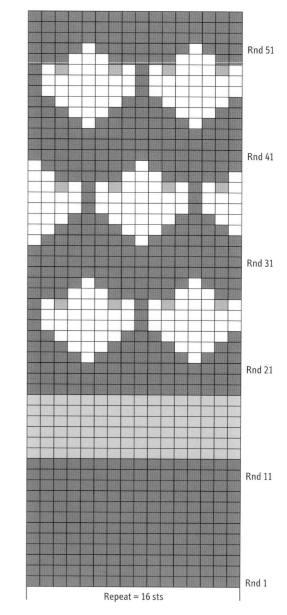

Rnd 51
Rnd 41
Rnd 31
Rnd 21
Rnd 11
Rnd 1

Repeat = 16 sts

 = Gray-blue Heather = Fern
= Super White = Ice Blue

PATTERN STITCHES

RIBBING

All rnds: (K2, p2) around.

STOCKINETTE STITCH (ST ST)

Working back and forth, knit RS rows, purl WS rows.
In the round, knit all rounds.

GARTER STITCH

Working back and forth, knit every row.
In the round, *knit 1 rnd, purl 1 rnd; rep from *.

CHART NOTES

Charts 1 and 2 are worked in St st in the round. Each square represents one stitch and each row in the chart represents one round or row of knitting. When changing colors, strand the unused yarn loosely on the back of the work, making sure the tension remains even. To avoid long floats, twist the working yarns around each other after every 2 to 3 stitches. Charts 1 and 2 both have repeats of 16 sts; Chart 1 is worked over 53 rnds and Chart 2 is worked over 54 rnds.

INSTRUCTIONS

With Ice Blue, CO 64 sts. Divide sts evenly on 4 dpns and join to work in the round, being careful not to twist sts.

CUFF

Work 6 rnds in Ribbing then change to Gray-blue and work another 17 rnds.

LEG

Begin working Chart 1, working 4 repeats of 16 sts around. The end of the rnd is between needles 1 and 4. Work all 53 rnds of Chart 1 (approx 6¼ in / 16 cm).

DUTCH HEEL (SEE PAGE 92)

Continue repeating chart rows 48-53 for Check Pattern and, *at the same time,* begin working the heel back and forth over the 32 sts on needles 1 and 4 as follows:
Work the first and last 4 sts of each row in garter st, and the middle 24 sts in St st. Work until 24 rows have been completed (approx 2¼ in / 6 cm).

TURN THE HEEL

With Gray-blue, follow basic instructions for turning a Dutch heel, working until decreases are made with the 2 sts before and after the center 8 sts—10 sts rem in heel.

INSTEP SHAPING

Continuing with Gray-blue, return to knitting in the round, picking up and knitting 14 sts along each side of the heel flap plus 1 extra st on each side between the heel and the instep sts. Needles 2 and 3 have 16 sts each, and needles 1 and 4 now have 20 sts each—72 sts total. The end of the rnd is between needles 1 and 4.

Begin working Chart 2 and, *at the same time*, dec as follows:
Next rnd: Knit around.
Dec rnd: Knit to last 3 sts on ndl 1, k2tog, k1; knit across needles 2 and 3; on ndl 4, k1, ssk, knit to end of rnd.
Repeat dec rnd every 3rd rnd 3 times—64 sts rem.

FOOT

Work until all 54 rows of Chart 2 have been completed (approx 6 in / 15 cm).

TOE

With Ice Blue, work in St st.
Rnd 1: Knit.
Dec rnd: *Knit to last 3 sts on ndl 1, k2tog, k1; on ndl 2, k1, ssk, knit to end of needle; rep from * on needles 3 and 4.
Repeat dec rnd every 3rd rnd 2 times, on every other rnd once, and then every rnd 9 times—12 sts rem.

FINISHING

Break the yarn and run the tail through the remaining sts. Pull gently to fasten off. Weave in ends neatly on WS.

Make a second sock the same way.

Colorful Bellflowers

LEVEL OF DIFFICULTY
Intermediate

SIZE
Women's large/
men's medium

MATERIALS
Yarn:

Fingering (CYCA #1)

Austermann Royal (60%
Merino wool/20% nylon/
10% cashmere/10% silk;
219 yd / 200 m/50 g),
Bottle Green (#26), 10 g

Schoeller + Stahl Fortissima
Socka (75% wool/25%
nylon; 229 yd / 209 m/50g),
Yellow (#1007), 20 g

Regia 4-ply (75% wool/
25% nylon; 229 yd / 210
m/50 g), Lavender (#1988),
Jaffa Orange (#1259) and
Bright Red (#2054), 20 g
each

Regia Extra Twist Merino
(75% wool/25% nylon;
229 yd / 210 m/50 g),
Navy Blue (#9356), 20 g

Needles: Set of 5 dpn
U.S. size 0 (2 mm) or size
needed to obtain gauge.

GAUGE
29 sts and 34½ rnds =
4 x 4 in (10 x 10 cm) over
Chart 1

30½ sts and 37½ rnds =
4 x 4 in (10 x 10 cm) over
Chart 2

■ = Navy Blue
□ = Yellow
▨ = Jaffa Orange
■ = Bright Red
▦ = Lavender

Chart 1

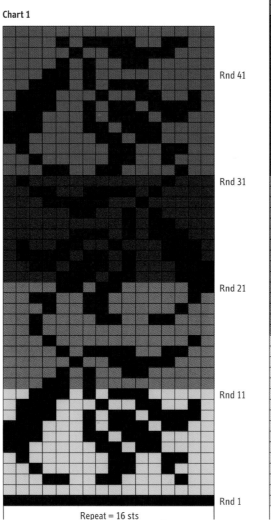

Rnd 41

Rnd 31

Rnd 21

Rnd 11

Rnd 1

Repeat = 16 sts

Chart 2

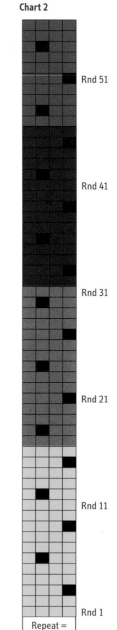

Rnd 51

Rnd 41

Rnd 31

Rnd 21

Rnd 11

Rnd 1

Repeat =
4 sts

PATTERN STITCHES

RIBBING
All rnds: (K2, p2) around.

STOCKINETTE STITCH (ST ST)
Working back and forth, knit RS rows,
purl WS rows.
In the round, knit all rounds.

GARTER STITCH
Working back and forth, knit every row.

CHART NOTES
Charts 1 and 2 are worked in St st in the
round. Each square represents one
stitch and each row in the chart represents one round or row of knitting.
When changing colors, strand the
unused yarn loosely on the back of the
work, making sure the tension remains
even. To avoid long floats, twist the
working yarns around each other after
every 2 to 3 stitches. Chart 1 has a
repeat of 16 sts worked over 45 rnds
and Chart 2 has a repeat of 4 sts
worked over 56 rnds.

INSTRUCTIONS

With Navy Blue, CO 64 sts. Divide sts
evenly on 4 dpns and join to work in the
round, being careful not to twist sts.

CUFF

Work 24 rnds (approx 2 in / 5.5 cm) in Ribbing.

LEG

Begin working Chart 1, working 4 repeats of 16 sts around. The end of the rnd is between needles 1 and 4. Work all 45 rnds of Chart 1 (approx 5 in / 13 cm).

DUTCH HEEL (SEE PAGE 92)

With Bottle Green, work the heel back and forth over the 32 sts on needles 1 and 4 as follows: Work the first and last 3 sts of each row in garter st, and the middle 26 sts in St st. Work until 26 rows have been completed (approx 2 in / 5 cm).

TURNING THE HEEL

With Bottle Green, follow basic instructions for turning a Dutch heel, working until decreases are made with the 2 sts before and after the center 12 sts—14 sts rem in heel.

INSTEP SHAPING

With Yellow, return to knitting in the round, picking up and knitting 13 sts along each side of the heel flap plus 1 extra st on each side between the heel and the instep sts. Needles 2 and 3 have 16 sts each, and needles 1 and 4 now have 21 sts each—74 sts total. The end of the rnd is between needles 1 and 4.
Begin working Chart 2 and, *at the same time*, dec as follows:
Knit 3 rnds even.
Dec rnd: Knit to last 3 sts on ndl 1, k2tog, k1; knit across needles 2 and 3; on ndl 4, k1, ssk, knit to end of rnd.
Repeat dec rnd every 3rd rnd 4 times—64 sts rem.

FOOT

Work even until all 56 rnds of Chart 2 are complete (approx 6 in / 15 cm).

TOE

With Bottle Green work in St st.
Rnd 1: Knit.
Dec rnd: *Knit to last 3 sts on ndl 1, k2tog, k1; on ndl 2, k1, ssk, knit to end of needle; rep from * on needles 3 and 4.
Repeat dec rnd every other rnd 5 times, then every rnd 7 times—12 sts rem.

FINISHING

Break the yarn and run the tail through the remaining sts. Pull gently to fasten off. Weave in ends neatly on WS.

Make a second sock the same way.

Tulips and Ornaments

LEVEL OF DIFFICULTY
Intermediate

SIZE
Women's x-large/men's large

MATERIALS
Yarn:

Fingering (CYCA #1)

Regia 4-ply (75% wool/25% nylon; 229 yd / 210 m/50 g), Black (#2066), 30 g, White (#600), Burgundy (#315), 20 g each and Cherry (#2002), 10 g

Regia Extra Twist Merino (75% wool/25% nylon; 229 yd / 210 m/50 g), Petrol Blue (#9357), 10 g

Schoeller + Stahl Fortissima (75% wool/25% nylon; 229 yd / 209 m/50 g), Light Gray (#1094), 20 g and Olive heather (#1089), 10 g

Needles: Set of 5 dpn U.S. size 0 (2 mm) or size needed to obtain gauge.

GAUGE
30½ sts and 37½ rnds = 4 x 4 in (10 x 10 cm) over Chart 1

32 sts and 37½ rnds = 4 x 4 in (10 x 10 cm) over Chart 2

PATTERN STITCHES

RIBBING
All rnds: (K2, p2) around.

STOCKINETTE STITCH (ST ST)
Working back and forth, knit RS rows, purl WS rows. In the round, knit all rounds.

GARTER STITCH
Working back and forth, knit every row.

CHART NOTES
Charts 1 and 2 are worked in St st in the round. Each square represents one stitch and each row in the chart represents one round or row of knitting. When changing colors, strand the unused yarn loosely on the back of the work, making sure the tension remains even. To avoid long floats, twist the working yarns around each other after every 2 to 3 stitches. Chart 1 has a repeat of 16 sts worked over 64 rounds and Chart 2 has a repeat of 8 sts worked over 7 rounds.

INSTRUCTIONS

With Black, CO 64 sts. Divide sts evenly on 4 dpns and join to work in the round, being careful not to twist sts.

CUFF
Work 24 rnds (approx 2¼ in / 5.5 cm) in Ribbing.

LEG
Begin working Chart 1, with 4 repeats of 16 sts around. The end of the rnd is between needles 1 and 4. Work all 64 rnds of Chart 1 (approx 6¾ in / 17 cm).

DUTCH HEEL (SEE PAGE 92)
With Black, work the heel back and forth over the 32 sts on needles 1 and 4 as follows:
Work the first and last 3 sts of each row in garter st, and the middle 26 sts in St st. Work in patt as est until 26 rows have been completed (approx 2¼ in / 5.5 cm).

TURNING THE HEEL

With Black, follow basic instructions for turning a Dutch heel, working until decreases are made with the 2 sts before and after the center 12 sts—14 sts rem in heel.

INSTEP SHAPING

Continuing with Black, return to knitting in the round, picking up and knitting 13 sts along each side of the heel flap plus 1 extra st on each side between the heel and the instep sts. Needles 2 and 3 have 16 sts each, and needles 1 and 4 now have 21 sts each—74 sts total. The end of the rnd is between needles 1 and 4.

Knit 3 rounds.

Dec rnd: Knit to last 3 sts on ndl 1, k2tog, k1; knit across needles 2 and 3; on ndl 4, k1, ssk, knit to end of rnd. Repeat dec rnd every 3rd rnd 4 times—64 sts rem.

FOOT

With Black, work in St st for 14 rnds until foot measures approx 1¼ in / 3.5 cm), then work all 7 rnds of Chart 2, followed by rnds 26-49 of Chart 1—31 rnds total (approx 3¾ in / 8.5 cm).

TOE

With Burgundy, work in St st.

Knit 3 rnds.

Dec rnd: *Knit to last 3 sts on ndl 1, k2tog, k1; on ndl 2, k1, ssk, knit to end of needle; rep from * on needles 3 and 4. Repeat dec rnd every other rnd 5 times, then every rnd 7 times—12 sts rem.

FINISHING

Break the yarn and run the tail through the remaining sts. Pull gently to fasten off. Weave in ends neatly on WS.

Make a second sock the same way.

Chart 1

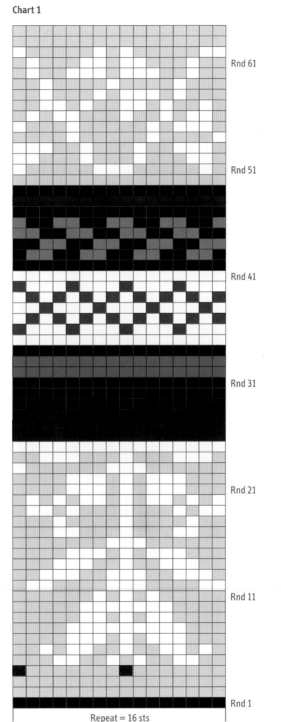

Rnd 61
Rnd 51
Rnd 41
Rnd 31
Rnd 21
Rnd 11
Rnd 1

Repeat = 16 sts

= Black
= Light Gray
= Burgundy
= White
= Petrol Blue
= Cherry
= Olive Heather

Chart 2

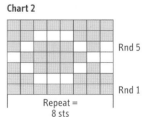

Rnd 5
Rnd 1

Repeat = 8 sts

Hidden Forget-Me-Nots

LEVEL OF DIFFICULTY
Easy

SIZE
Women's medium/men's small

MATERIALS
Yarn:

Fingering (CYCA #1)

Regia 4-ply (75% wool/25% nylon; 229 yd / 210 m/50 g), Royal Blue (#2000), 30 g, Flannel heather (#33), 20 g, Ice Blue (#2018), Yellow (#2041) and Fern (#1092), 10 g each

Lana Grossa Meilenweit 50 (80% wool/20% nylon; 230 yd / 210 m/50 g), Medium Blue (#1335), 20 g

Needles: Set of 5 dpn U.S. size 0 (2 mm) or size needed to obtain gauge.

GAUGE
31 sts and 40½ rnds = 4 x 4 in (10 x 10 cm) in St st

30½ sts and 36 rnds = 4 x 4 in (10 x 10 cm) over Charted Pattern

Chart

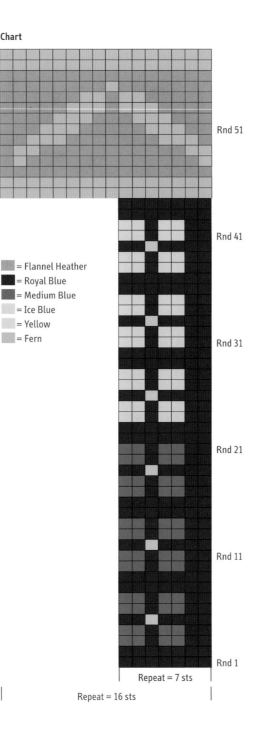

Rnd 51

Rnd 41

= Flannel Heather
= Royal Blue
= Medium Blue
= Ice Blue
= Yellow
= Fern

Rnd 31

Rnd 21

Rnd 11

Rnd 1

Repeat = 7 sts

Repeat = 16 sts

PATTERN STITCHES

RIBBING
All rnds: (K2, p2) around.

STOCKINETTE STITCH (ST ST)
Working back and forth, knit RS rows, purl WS rows. In the round, knit all rounds.

GARTER STITCH
Working back and forth, knit every row.

CHART NOTES
Chart is worked in St st in the round. Each square represents one stitch and each row in the chart represents one round or row of knitting. When changing colors, strand the unused yarn loosely on the back of the work, making sure tension remains even tension. To avoid long floats, twist the working yarns around each other after every 2 to 3 stitches. The Forget-Me-Not Pattern has a repeat of 7 sts worked over chart rows 1-44 and the Leaf Pattern has a repeat of 16 sts worked over chart rows 45-58.

INSTRUCTIONS

With Flannel heather, CO 64 sts. Divide sts evenly on 4 dpns and join to work in the round, being careful not to twist sts.

CUFF
Work 24 rnds (approx 2¼ in / 6 cm) in striped Ribbing as follows:
3 rnds Flannel heather, *4 rnds Royal Blue, 4 rnds Flannel heather; rep from * once more and then work 4 rnds Royal Blue and 1 rnd Flannel heather. End with 1 more rnd Flannel heather.

LEG

Begin working Chart 1, working 9 repeats of 7 sts around and ending the round with 1 additional st of Royal Blue (3 blue sts together, including the 2 at the beg of the rnd). The end of the rnd is between needles 1 and 4. After rnd 44, work 4 repeats of 16 sts around. Work until all 58 rnds of Chart 1 are complete (approx 6¼ in / 16 cm).

DUTCH HEEL (SEE PAGE 92)

With Royal Blue, work the heel back and forth over the 32 sts on needles 1 and 4 as follows: Work the first and last 4 sts of each row in garter st, and the middle 24 sts in St st. Work in patt as est until 28 rows have been completed (approx 2¼ in / 6 cm).

TURNING THE HEEL

With Royal Blue, follow basic instructions for turning a Dutch heel, working until decreases are made with the 2 sts before and after the center 10 sts—12 sts rem in heel.

INSTEP SHAPING

Continuing with Royal Blue, return to knitting in the round, picking up and knitting 13 sts along each side of the heel flap plus 1 extra st on each side between the heel and the instep sts. Needles 2 and 3 have 16 sts each, and needles 1 and 4 now have 20 sts each—72 sts total. The end of the rnd is between needles 1 and 4.
Next rnd: Knit around.
Dec rnd: Knit to last 3 sts on ndl 1, k2tog, k1; knit across needles 2 and 3; on ndl 4, k1, ssk, knit to end of rnd.
Repeat dec rnd every 3rd rnd 3 times—64 sts rem.

FOOT

Work even in St st for 16 rnds (approx 1½ in / 4 cm).

Work rows 10-28 of Chart, then with Royal Blue, work in St st for another 16 rnds (approx 1½ in / 4 cm), and finish with 2 rnds in Fern.

TOE

With Flannel heather work in St st.
Rnd 1: Knit.
Dec rnd: *Knit to last 3 sts on ndl 1, k2tog, k1; on ndl 2, k1, ssk, knit to end of needle; rep from * on needles 3 and 4.
Repeat dec rnd every 3rd rnd twice, then every other rnd once, and, finally, on every rnd 10 times—8 sts rem.

FINISHING

Break the yarn and run the tail through the remaining sts. Pull gently to fasten off. Weave in ends neatly on WS.

Make a second sock the same way.

Animals

Cats and fish stand out in bright colors against black backgrounds, while in the Ethno Look socks, the opposite is true and the background shimmers in warm earth tones, enlivening the exotic animal pictures.

EXOTIC FISH
Instructions page 46

PERUVIAN CATS
Instructions page 44

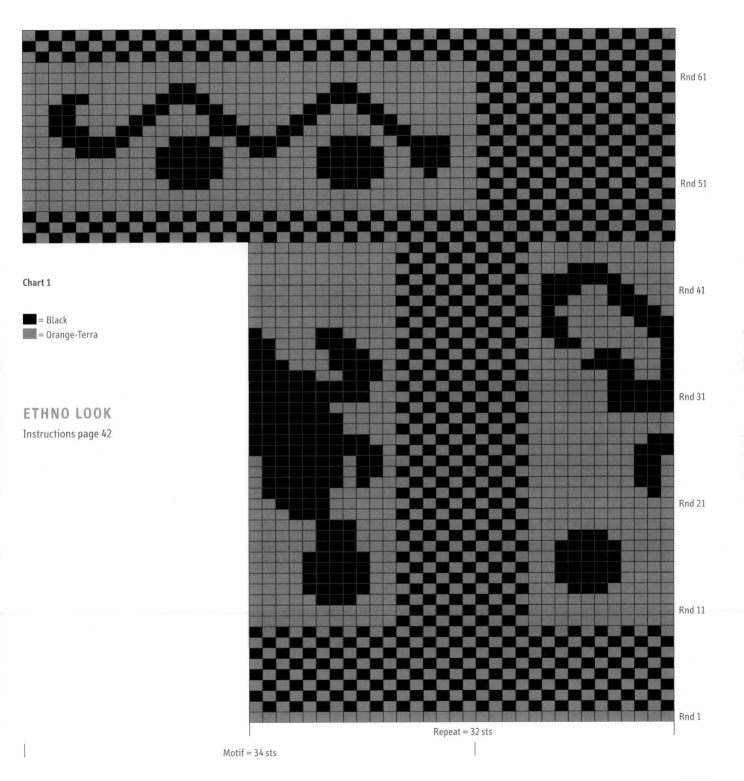

Chart 1

■ = Black
■ = Orange-Terra

ETHNO LOOK
Instructions page 42

Rnd 61

Rnd 51

Rnd 41

Rnd 31

Rnd 21

Rnd 11

Rnd 1

Repeat = 32 sts

Motif = 34 sts

Ethno Look

LEVEL OF DIFFICULTY
Experienced

SIZE
Women's small

MATERIALS
Yarn:

Fingering (CYCA #1)

Lana Grossa Meilenweit solo tono (80% wool/ 20% nylon; 459 yd / 420 m/100 g), Orange-Terra (#5220), 60g

Regia 4-ply (75% wool/ 25% nylon; 229 yd / 210 m/50 g), Black (#2066), 40 g

Needles: Set of 5 dpn U.S. size 0 (2 mm) or size needed to obtain gauge.

GAUGE
29 sts and 34 rnds = 4 x 4 in (10 x 10 cm) over Chart 1

32 sts and 36 rnds = 4 x 4 in (10 x 10 cm) over Chart 2

PATTERN STITCHES

STOCKINETTE STITCH (ST ST)

Working back and forth, knit RS rows, purl WS rows.

In the round, knit all rounds.

REVERSE STOCKINETTE STITCH (REV ST ST)

In the round, purl all rounds.

GARTER STITCH

Working back and forth, knit every row.

Chart 2

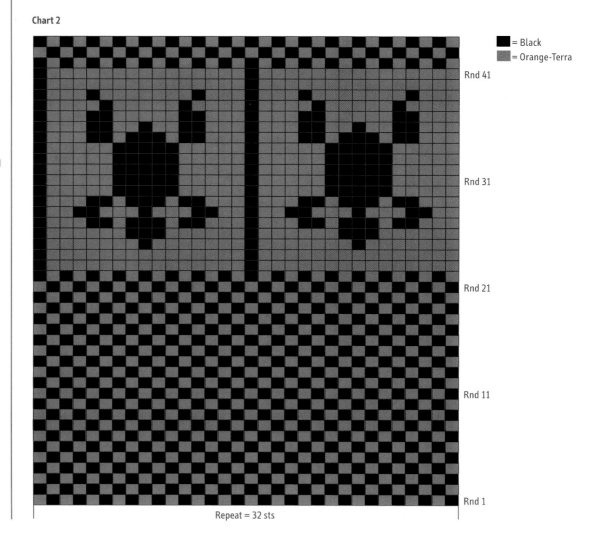

= Black
= Orange-Terra

Rnd 41

Rnd 31

Rnd 21

Rnd 11

Rnd 1

Repeat = 32 sts

CHART NOTES

Charts 1 and 2 are worked in St st in the round. Each square represents one stitch and each row in the chart represents one round or row of knitting. When changing colors, strand the unused yarn loosely on the back of the work, making sure the tension remains even. To avoid long floats, twist the working yarns around each other after every 2 to 3 stitches. Make sure you always carry the same color ahead (in the left hand if you are knitting with one color in each hand), or the pattern will be uneven. The pattern repeat is 32 stitches which is worked twice on the 64 sts in the rnd, but, for the serpent motif on rows 46-65 of Chart 1, the motif is worked only once, surrounded by the check stitch as shown in the chart.

INSTRUCTIONS

With Orange-Terra, CO 64 sts. Divide sts evenly on 4 dpns and join to work in the round, being careful not to twist sts.

CUFF

Work 20 rnds (approx 1¾ in / 4.5 cm) in St st and then purl 2 rnds.

LEG

Begin working Chart 1, working 2 repeats of 32 sts around. The end of the rnd is between needles 1 and 4. Work all 65 rnds of Chart 1 (approx 7½ in / 19 cm), working one 32-st repeat of the lizard motif on the front of the leg, and the second on the back of the leg. After row 45, work only 1 repeat of the serpent motif centered below the lizard motif on the front of the leg; work the rest of the round in the check patt as charted.

DUTCH HEEL (SEE PAGE 92)

With Orange-Terra, work the heel back and forth over the 32 sts on needles 1 and 4 as follows: Work the first and last 4 sts of each row in garter st, and the middle 24 sts in St st. Work in patt as est until 28 rows have been completed (approx 2¼ in / 5.5 cm).

TURN THE HEEL

With Orange-Terra, follow basic instructions for turning a Dutch heel, working until decreases are made with the 2 sts before and after the center 8 sts—10 sts rem in heel.

INSTEP SHAPING

Continuing with Orange-Terra, return to knitting in the round, picking up and knitting 13 sts along each side of the heel flap plus 1 extra st on each side between the heel and the instep sts. Needles 2 and 3 have 16 sts each, and needles 1 and 4 now have 19 sts each—70 sts total. The end of the rnd is between needles 1 and 4.
Begin working Chart 2, being careful to maintain check patt as est, and, *at the same time*, dec as follows:
Next rnd: Knit around.
Dec rnd: Knit to last 3 sts on ndl 1, k2tog, k1; knit across needles 2 and 3; on ndl 4, k1, ssk, knit to end of rnd.
Repeat dec rnd every 3rd rnd twice—64 sts rem.

FOOT

Work even for the foot and, after row 12 of Chart 2, begin working turtle motifs, being careful to align the pattern so one repeat of 32 sts is on top of the foot and the second repeat is on the sole. Continue until all 44 rnds of Chart 2 are complete (approx 5 in / 12.5 cm).

TOE

With Orange-Terra work in St st.
Rnd 1: Knit.
Dec rnd: *Knit to last 3 sts on ndl 1, k2tog, k1; on ndl 2, k1, ssk, knit to end of needle; rep from * on needles 3 and 4.
Repeat dec rnd every 3rd rnd twice, then every other rnd once, then ever round 9 times—12 sts rem.

FINISHING

Break the yarn and run the tail through the remaining sts. Pull gently to fasten off. Weave in ends neatly on WS.

Make a second sock the same way.

Peruvian Cats

LEVEL OF DIFFICULTY
Easy

SIZE
Women's medium/men's small

MATERIALS
Yarn:

Fingering (CYCA #1)

Regia 4-ply (75% wool/25% nylon; 229 yd / 210 m/50 g), Black (#2066), 50 g

Regia Extra Twist Merino (75% wool/25% nylon; 229 yd / 210 m/50 g), Red (#9353), 20 g

Lana Grossa Meilenweit 50 g (80% wool/20% nylon; 230 yd / 210 m/50 g), Pink (# 1313), 20g and Violet (#1336), 10 g

Needles: Set of 5 dpn U.S. size 1-2 (2.5 mm) or size needed to obtain gauge.

GAUGE
34½ sts and 44 rnds = 4 x 4 in (10 x 10 cm) in St st

30 sts and 36½ rnds = 4 x 4 in (10 x 10 cm) over Charted Pattern

PATTERN STITCHES

RIBBING
All rnds: (K2, p2) around.

STOCKINETTE STITCH (ST ST)
Working back and forth, knit RS rows, purl WS rows.
In the round, knit all rounds.

GARTER STITCH
Working back and forth, knit every row.

CHART NOTES
The charted pattern is worked in St st in the round. Each square represents one stitch and each row in the chart represents one round or row of knitting. When changing colors, strand the unused yarn loosely on the back of the work, making sure the tension remains even. To avoid long floats, twist the working yarns around each other after every 2 to 3 stitches. The chart has a repeat of 24 stitches worked over 68 rnds. Extra stitches are shown at the beginning and end of the rows in the chart so you can see how to align the pattern.

INSTRUCTIONS

With Black, CO 72 sts. Divide sts evenly on 4 dpns and join to work in the round, being careful not to twist sts.

CUFF
Work 23 rnds (approx 2¼ in / 5.5 cm) in Ribbing as follows: Work 3 rnds Black, 3 rnds Pink, and then work corrugated ribbing (k2 Pink, p2 Black), stranding the unused color behind the work.

LEG
Begin working Charted pattern, working 3 repeats of 24 sts around (remember the chart has extra stitches outside of the 24-st repeat which are only to illustrate the alignment of the pattern). The end of the rnd is between needles 1 and 4. Work all 68 rnds of Chart 1 (approx 7¼ in / 18.5 cm).

DUTCH HEEL (SEE PAGE 92)
With Red, work the heel back and forth over the 36 sts on needles 1 and 4 as follows:
Work the first and last 4 sts of each row in garter st, and the middle 28 sts in St st. Work in patt as est until 28 rows have been completed (approx 2¼ in / 5.5 cm).

TURNING THE HEEL
With Red, follow basic instructions for turning a Dutch heel, working until decreases are made with the 2 sts before and after the center 10 sts—12 sts rem in heel.

INSTEP SHAPING
Continuing with Red, return to knitting in the round, picking up and knitting 13 sts along each side of the heel flap plus 1 extra st on each side between the heel and the instep sts. Needles 2 and 3 have 18 sts each, and needles 1 and 4 now

Chart

have 20 sts each—76 sts total. The end of the rnd is between needles 1 and 4.

Knit 2 rnds even.

Dec rnd: Knit to last 3 sts on ndl 1, k2tog, k1; knit across needles 2 and 3; on ndl 4, k1, ssk, knit to end of rnd.

Repeat the last 3 rnds once more—72 sts rem.

Knit 1 rnd.

Change to Black.

FOOT

Work even in St st in Black for 60 rnds (approx 5½ in /13.5 cm).

TOE

Rnd 1: Knit.

Dec rnd: *Knit to last 3 sts on ndl 1, k2tog, k1; on ndl 2, k1, ssk, knit to end of needle; rep from * on needles 3 and 4.

Repeat dec rnd every other rnd 4 times, then every rnd 10 times—12 sts rem.

FINISHING

Break the yarn and run the tail through the remaining sts. Pull gently to fasten off. Weave in ends neatly on WS.

Make a second sock the same way.

- ■ = Black
- ■ = Red
- ■ = Violet
- ■ = Pink

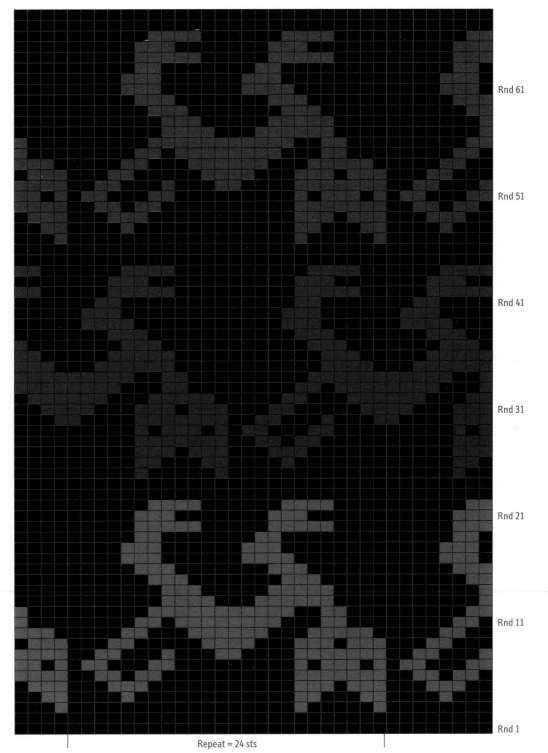

Rnd 61

Rnd 51

Rnd 41

Rnd 31

Rnd 21

Rnd 11

Rnd 1

Repeat = 24 sts

Exotic Fish

LEVEL OF DIFFICULTY
Intermediate

SIZE
Women's medium/men's small

MATERIALS
Yarn:

Fingering (CYCA #1)

Regia 4-ply (75% wool/25% nylon; 229 yd / 210 m/50 g), Black (#2066), 30 g, Bright Red (#2054), Royal (#540) and Lavender (#1988), 20 g each, Cardinal (#1078), Jaffa Orange (#1259), Yellow (#2041), Fern (#1092), Leaf Green (#2082) and Ice Blue (#2018), 10 g each

Regia Extra Twist Merino (75% wool/25% nylon; 229 yd / 210 m/50 g), Petrol Blue (#9357), 10 g

Needles: Set of 5 dpn U.S. size 0 (2 mm) or size needed to obtain gauge.

GAUGE
30 sts and 38 rnds = 4 x 4 in (10 x 10 cm) over Chart 1

32 sts and 37 rnds = 4 x 4 in (10 x 10 cm) over Chart 2

Chart 1

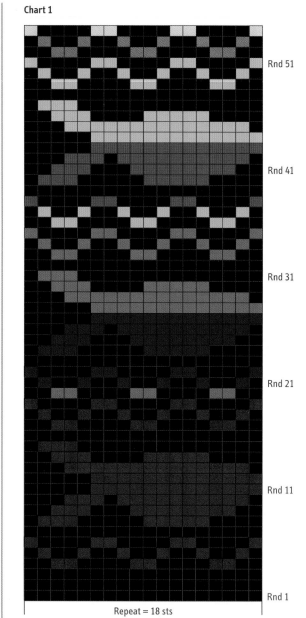

Rnd 51
Rnd 41
Rnd 31
Rnd 21
Rnd 11
Rnd 1

Repeat = 18 sts

■ = Black
☐ = Yellow
■ = Jaffa Orange
■ = Bright Red
■ = Lavender
■ = Royal Blue
■ = Leaf Green
■ = Fern
☐ = Ice Blue
■ = Petrol Blue
■ = Cardinal

Chart 2

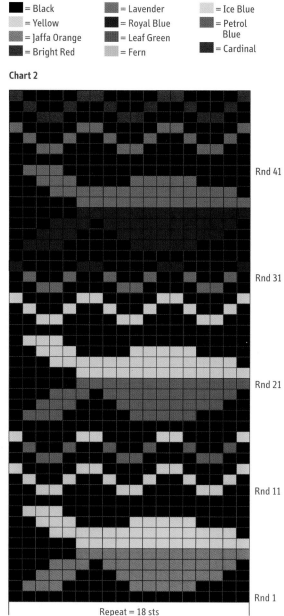

Rnd 41
Rnd 31
Rnd 21
Rnd 11
Rnd 1

Repeat = 18 sts

PATTERN STITCHES

RIBBING
All rnds: (K2, p2) around.

STOCKINETTE STITCH (ST ST)
Working back and forth, knit RS rows, purl WS rows.
In the round, knit all rounds.

CHART NOTES
Charts 1 and 2 are worked in St st in the round. Each square represents one stitch and each row in the chart represents one round or row of knitting. When changing colors, strand the unused yarn loosely on the back of the work, making sure the tension remains even. To avoid long floats, twist the working yarns around each other after every 2 to 3 stitches. Charts 1 and 2 have a repeat of 18 sts. Chart 1 is worked over 54 rnds on the leg and Chart 2 is worked over 48 rnds on the foot.

INSTRUCTIONS

With Black, CO 72 sts. Divide sts evenly on 4 dpns and join to work in the round, being careful not to twist sts.

CUFF
Work 23 rnds (approx 2¼ in / 5.5 cm) in Ribbing as follows:
Work 3 rnds in Black, then work corrugated ribbing (k2 Black, p2 Red), stranding the unused color behind the work.

LEG
Begin working Chart 1, working 4 repeats of 18

sts around. The end of the rnd is between needles 1 and 4. Work all 54 rnds of Chart 1 (approx 5¼ in / 14 cm).

SHORT-ROW HEEL (SEE PAGES 90-91)
Using Black for the first row, then changing to Yellow, work the heel back and forth in St st over the 32 sts on needles 1 and 4 as follows (see basic short-row heel technique, pages 90-91): Divide the heel stitches into 3 sections with 10 sts in the center and 13 sts on each side. Work decreasing short-row section, using the double-stitch technique for working turns. When 10 sts rem in center, knit 2 rounds on all four needles, working both loops of each double stitch together as one stitch. End the second round at the beginning of the middle section of the heel. Change to Jaffa Orange and work increasing-row section, using the double-stitch technique and completing heel as described in the basic instructions.

FOOT
Return to working in the round, picking up the double loops and knitting them together on first rnd—72 sts.
Work all 48 rnds of Chart 2 (approx 5 in / 13 cm).

TOE
With Bright Red work in St st.
Knit 3 rnds.
Dec rnd: *Knit to last 3 sts on ndl 1, k2tog, k1; on ndl 2, k1, ssk, knit to end of needle; rep from * again on needles 3 and 4.
Repeat dec rnd every 3rd rnd twice, then every rnd 12 times—12 sts rem.

FINISHING
Break the yarn and run the tail through the remaining sts. Pull gently to fasten off. Weave in ends neatly on WS.

Make a second sock the same way.

Stars

Colorful stars, wintry snowflakes, and geometric ornaments make these socks unique. Whether in cool blue, green, and violet tones with black highlights or warm oranges and yellows, there's no denying that knitting these socks will be fun.

STAR FIELD
Instructions page 56

COLORFUL STAR PATTERN
Instructions page 58

LOZENGES
Instructions page 60

SNOWFLAKES
Instructions page 62

Star Field

LEVEL OF DIFFICULTY
Intermediate

SIZE
Women's medium/men's small

MATERIALS
Yarn:

Fingering (CYCA #1)

Regia Hand-dye Effect (70% wool/25% nylon/ 5% acrylic; 459 yd / 420 m/100g), Jasper (#6558), 70 g

Regia 4-ply (75% wool/25% nylon; 229 yd / 210 m/50 g), Ice Blue (#2018), 10 g

Regia Extra Twist Merino (75% wool/25% nylon; 229 yd / 210 m/50 g), Petrol Blue (#9357) and Violet (#9354), 10 g each

Lana Grossa Meilenweit 100 Merino (80% wool/ 20% nylon; 460 yd / 421 m/100 g), Green (#2018), 20 g

Needles: Set of 5 dpn U.S. size 0 (2 mm) or size needed to obtain gauge.

GAUGE
30 sts and 37½ rnds = 4 x 4 in (10 x 10 cm) over Chart 1

31½ sts and 37½ rnds = 4 x 4 in (10 x 10 cm) over Chart 2

PATTERN STITCHES

RIBBING

All rnds: (K2, p2) around.

STOCKINETTE STITCH (ST ST)

Working back and forth, knit RS rows, purl WS rows. In the round, knit all rounds.

GARTER STITCH

Working back and forth, knit every row.

CHART NOTES

Charts 1 and 2 are worked in St st in the round. Each square represents one stitch and each row in the chart represents one round or row of knitting. When changing colors, strand the unused yarn loosely on the back of the work, making sure the tension remains even. To avoid long floats, twist the working yarns around each other after every 2 to 3 stitches. Charts 1 and 2 have a repeat of 18 sts. Chart 1 is worked over 56 rnds and Chart 2 is worked over 60 rnds.

INSTRUCTIONS

With Jasper, CO 72 sts. Divide sts evenly on 4 dpns and join to work in the round, being careful not to twist sts.

CUFF

Work 24 rnds (approx 2 in / 5 cm) in Ribbing.

LEG

Begin working Chart 1, working 4 repeats of 18 sts around. The end of the rnd is between needles 1 and 4. Work all 56 rnds of Chart 1 (approx 6 in / 15 cm).

DUTCH HEEL (SEE PAGE 92)

With Jasper, work the heel back and forth over the 36 sts on needles 1 and 4 as follows:

Work the first and last 4 sts of each row in garter st, and the middle 28 sts in St st. Work in patt as est until 26 rows have been completed (approx 2 in / 5 cm).

TURNING THE HEEL

With Jasper, follow basic instructions for turning a Dutch heel, working until decreases are made with the 2 sts before and after the center 10 sts—12 sts rem in heel.

INSTEP SHAPING

Continuing with Jasper, return to knitting in the round, picking up and knitting 13 sts along each side of the heel flap plus 1 extra st on each side between the heel and the instep sts. Needles 2 and 3 have 18 sts each, and needles 1 and 4 now have 20 sts each—76 sts total. The end of the rnd is between needles 1 and 4.

Next rnd: Knit around.

Dec rnd: Knit to last 3 sts on ndl 1, k2tog, k1; knit across needles 2 and 3; on ndl 4, k1, ssk, knit to end of rnd.

Repeat last 2 rnds once
more—72 sts rem.

FOOT

Work all 60 rnds of Chart
2 (approx 6¼ in / 16 cm).

TOE

With Jasper, work in St st.
Rnd 1: Knit.
Dec rnd: *Knit to last 3 sts
on ndl 1, k2tog, k1; on ndl
2, k1, ssk, knit to end of
needle; rep from * on
needles 3 and 4.
Repeat dec rnd every
other rnd twice, then
every rnd 12 times—12
sts rem.

FINISHING

Break the yarn and run
the tail through the
remaining sts. Pull gently
to fasten off. Weave in
ends neatly on WS.

Make a second sock the
same way.

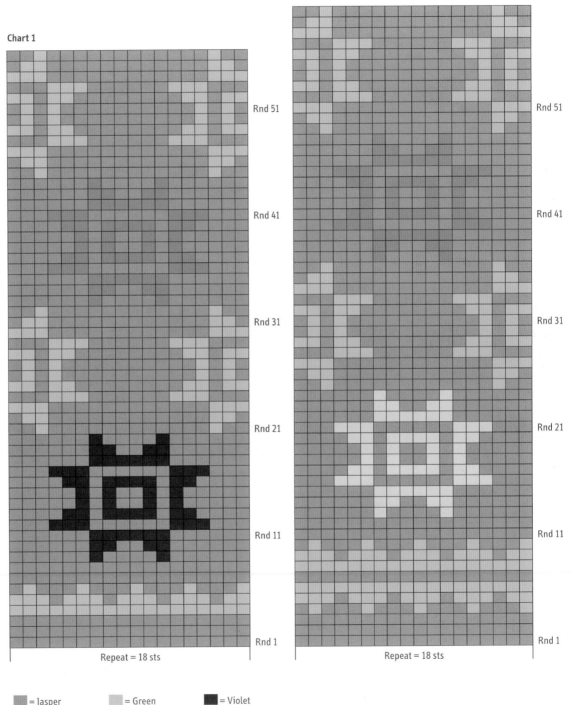

Chart 1

Rnd 51

Rnd 41

Rnd 31

Rnd 21

Rnd 11

Rnd 1

Repeat = 18 sts

Chart 2

Rnd 51

Rnd 41

Rnd 31

Rnd 21

Rnd 11

Rnd 1

Repeat = 18 sts

= Jasper   = Green   = Violet

= Petrol Blue   = Ice Blue

Colorful Star Pattern

LEVEL OF DIFFICULTY
Easy

SIZE
Teen large/women's small

MATERIALS
Yarn:

Fingering (CYCA #1)

Regia 4-ply (75% wool/
25% nylon; 229 yd /
210 m/50 g), White (#600),
30 g

Lana Grossa Meilenweit
100 Stile (80% wool/
20% nylon; 459 yd /
420 m/100 g), Red/Purple/
Brown/Rust (#8016), 30 g

Needles: Set of 5 dpn U.S.
size 0 (2 mm) or size needed
to obtain gauge.

GAUGE
34 sts and 46 rnds =
4 x 4 in (10 x 10 cm) in
St st

32 sts and 36 rnds =
4 x 4 in (10 x 10 cm) over
Charted Pattern

PATTERN STITCHES

RIBBING
All rnds: (K2, p2) around.

STOCKINETTE STITCH (ST ST)
Working back and forth, knit RS rows, purl WS rows
In the round, knit all rounds.

GARTER STITCH
Working back and forth, knit every row.

Chart

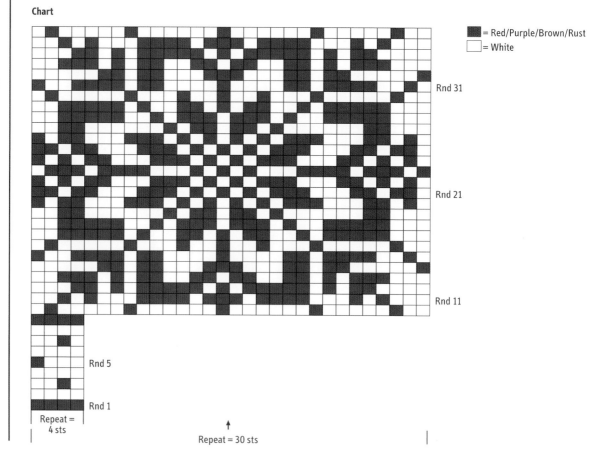

Rnd 31

Rnd 21

Rnd 11

Rnd 5

Rnd 1

Repeat =
4 sts

↑
Repeat = 30 sts

CHART NOTES

The charted pattern is worked in St st in the round. Each square represents one stitch and each row in the chart represents one round or row of knitting. When changing colors, strand the unused yarn loosely on the back of the work, making sure the tension remains even. To avoid long floats, twist the working yarns around each other after every 2 to 3 stitches. The Star Motif has a repeat of 30 sts and is worked over rows 9-36 of the chart. The small pattern has a repeat of 4 stitches and is worked over rows 1-8 of the chart.

■ = Red/Purple/Brown/Rust
□ = White

INSTRUCTIONS

With Red/Purple/Brown/Rust, CO 60 sts. Divide sts evenly on 4 dpns and join to work in the round, being careful not to twist sts.

CUFF
Work 24 rnds (approx 2 in / 5 cm) in Ribbing.

LEG
Begin working Chart 1, aligning the pattern so the one repeat of 30 sts spans needles 1 and 2 and the other repeat spans needles 3 and 4 and the Star Motifs are aligned on the sides of the sock leg. Work all 36 rnds of the chart, then work rnds 1–8 once more (44 rnds total, approx 5¾ in / 12 cm).

DUTCH HEEL (SEE PAGE 92)
With Red/Purple/ Brown/Rust, work the heel back and forth over the 30 sts on needles 1 and 4 as follows:
Work the first and last 3 sts of each row in garter st, and the middle 24 sts in St st. Work in patt as est until 24 rows have been completed (approx 2 in / 5 cm).

TURNING THE HEEL
With Red/Purple/ Brown/Rust, follow basic instructions for turning a Dutch heel, working until decreases are made with the 2 sts before and after the center 10 sts—12 sts rem in heel.

INSTEP SHAPING
With White, return to knitting in the round, picking up and knitting 12 sts along each side of the heel flap plus 1 extra st on each side between the heel and the instep sts. Needles 2 and 3 have

15 sts each, and needles 1 and 4 now have 19 sts each—68 sts total. The end of the rnd is between needles 1 and 4.
Next rnd: Knit around.
Dec rnd: Knit to last 3 sts on ndl 1, k2tog, k1; knit across needles 2 and 3; on ndl 4, k1, ssk, knit to end of rnd.
Repeat dec rnd every 3rd rnd 3 times—60 sts rem.

FOOT
With White, work in St st for 36 rnds (approx 3¼ in / 8 cm).

TOE
With Red/Purple/ Brown/Rust work in St st. Knit 5 rnds.

Dec rnd: *Knit to last 3 sts on ndl 1, k2tog, k1; on ndl 2, k1, ssk, knit to end of needle; rep from * on needles 3 and 4.
Repeat dec rnd every other rnd 5 times, then every rnd 6 times—12 sts rem.

FINISHING
Break the yarn and run the tail through the remaining sts. Pull gently to fasten off. Weave in ends neatly on WS.

Make a second sock the same way.

Lozenges

LEVEL OF DIFFICULTY
Intermediate

SIZE
Women's medium/men's small

MATERIALS
Yarn:

Fingering (CYCA #1)

Regia 4-ply (75% wool/ 25% nylon; 229 yd / 210 m/50 g), Yellow (#2041), Natural (#1992), Lemon (#2019) and Jaffa Orange (#1259), 30 g each

Austermann Step Classic (75% wool/25% nylon; 460 yd / 421 m/100 g), Beige (#1001), Red-brown (#1006) and Loden Green (#1003), 25 g each

Needles: Set of 5 dpn U.S. size 0 (2 mm) or size needed to obtain gauge.

GAUGE
30 sts and 37 rnds = 4 x 4 in (10 x 10 cm) over Chart 1

32 sts and 33½ rnds = 4 x 4 in (10 x 10 cm) over Chart 2

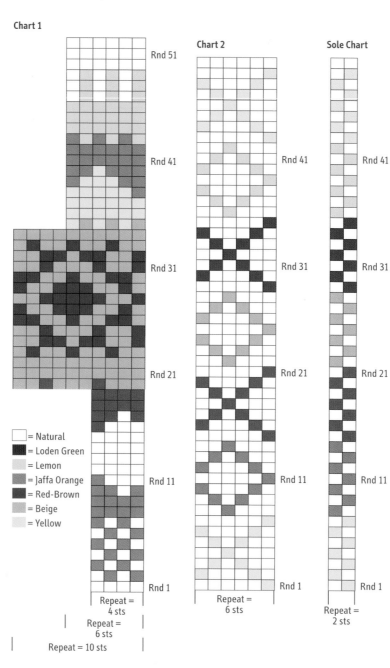

Chart 1

Chart 2

Sole Chart

Rnd 51

Rnd 41

Rnd 31

Rnd 21

Rnd 11

Rnd 1

= Natural
= Loden Green
= Lemon
= Jaffa Orange
= Red-Brown
= Beige
= Yellow

Repeat = 4 sts
Repeat = 6 sts
Repeat = 10 sts

Repeat = 6 sts

Repeat = 2 sts

PATTERN STITCHES

RIBBING
All rnds: (K2, p2) around.

STOCKINETTE STITCH (ST ST)
Working back and forth, knit RS rows, purl WS rows.
In the round, knit all rounds.

GARTER STITCH
Working back and forth, knit every row.

CHART NOTES
All charts are worked in St st in the round. Each square represents one stitch and each row in the chart represents one round or row of knitting. When changing colors, strand the unused yarn loosely on the back of the work, making sure the tension remains even. To avoid long floats, twist the working yarns around each other after every 2 to 3 stitches. Chart 1 has a repeat of 4 sts in rows 1-19, a repeat of 10 sts in rows 20-34, and a repeat of 6 sts in rows 35-52. Chart 2 has a repeat of 6 sts and is worked over 50 rnds on the top of the foot. Chart 3 has a repeat of 2 sts and is worked over 50 rnds on the sole of the foot.

SOLE PATTERN

The sole pattern is a 2 stitch repeat and is worked continuously on the sole of the sock after the heel turn is complete.

INSTRUCTIONS

With Yellow, CO 60 sts. Divide sts evenly on 4 dpns and join to work in the round, being careful not to twist sts.

CUFF

Work 24 rnds (approx 2¼ in / 5.5 cm) in Ribbing, then knit 1 rnd.

LEG

Begin working Chart 1. The end of the rnd falls between two of the Large Star motifs and is between needles 1 and 4. Work all 52 rnds of Chart 1 (approx 5½ in / 14 cm).

DUTCH HEEL (SEE PAGE 92)

With Red-brown, work the heel back and forth over the 30 sts on needles 1 and 4 as follows: Work the first and last 3 sts of each row in garter st, and the middle 24 sts in St st. Work in patt as est until 26 rows have been completed (approx 2¼ in / 6 cm).

TURNING THE HEEL

With Beige, follow basic instructions for turning a Dutch heel, working until decreases are made with the 2 sts before and after the center 10 sts—12 sts rem in heel.

INSTEP SHAPING

With Natural, return to knitting in the round, picking up and knitting 13 sts along each side of the heel flap plus 1 extra st on each side between the heel and the instep sts. Needles 2 and 3 have 15 sts each, and needles 1 and 4 now have 20 sts each—70 sts total. The end of the rnd is between needles 1 and 4.
Next rnd: Knit around.
Dec rnd: Knit to last 3 sts on ndl 1, k2tog, k1; knit across needles 2 and 3; on ndl 4, k1, ssk, knit to end of rnd.

Repeat dec rnd every 3rd rnd 4 times—60 sts rem.

FOOT

Work Chart 2 on needles 2 and 3 and Chart 3 (sole pattern) on needles 1 and 4 until all 50 rnds of charts are complete (approx 6 in / 15 cm).

TOE

With Jaffa, work in St st.
Dec rnd: *Knit to last 3 sts on ndl 1, k2tog, k1; on ndl 2, k1, ssk, knit to end of needle; rep from * on needles 3 and 4.
Next rnd: Knit.
Repeat dec rnd every other rnd 5 times, then every rnd 6 times—12 sts rem.

FINISHING

Break the yarn and run the tail through the remaining sts. Pull gently to fasten off. Weave in ends neatly on WS.

Make a second sock the same way.

Snowflakes

LEVEL OF DIFFICULTY
Easy

SIZE
Women's medium/
men's small

MATERIALS
Yarn:

Fingering (CYCA #1)

Lana Grossa Meilenweit
Stile (80% wool/20%
nylon; 459 yd / 420 m/100
g), Green-Orange (#8001),
70 g

Regia 4-ply (75%
wool/25% nylon; 229 yd /
210 m/50 g), White (#600),
20 g

Needles: Set of 5 dpn U.S.
size 0 (2 mm) or size needed
to obtain gauge.

GAUGE
32 sts and 42 rnds =
4 x 4 in (10 x 10 cm) in St st

29 sts and 33 rnds =
4 x 4 in (10 x 10 cm) over
Charted Pattern

Chart

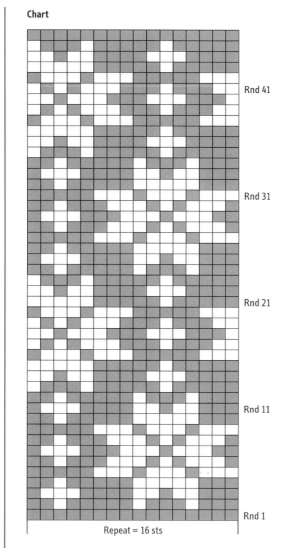

Rnd 41

Rnd 31

Rnd 21

Rnd 11

Rnd 1

Repeat = 16 sts

 = White
= Green-Orange

PATTERN STITCHES

RIBBING
All rnds: (K2, p2) around.

STOCKINETTE STITCH (ST ST)
Working back and forth, knit RS rows, purl WS rows.
In the round, knit all rounds.

GARTER STITCH
Working back and forth, knit every row.

CHART NOTES
The charted pattern is worked in St st in the round. Each
square represents one stitch and each row in the chart represents one round or row of knitting. When changing colors,
strand the unused yarn loosely on the back of the work,
making sure the tension remains even. To avoid long floats,
twist the working yarns around each other after every 2 to 3
stitches. Chart has a repeat of 16 sts worked over 46 rounds.

INSTRUCTIONS

With Green-Orange, CO 64 sts. Divide sts evenly on 4 dpns
and join to work in the round, being careful not to twist sts.

CUFF
Work 24 rnds (approx 2¼ in / 5.5 cm) in Ribbing.

LEG
Begin working Chart 1, working 4 repeats of 16 sts around.
The end of the rnd is between needles 1 and 4. Work all 46
rnds (approx 5½ in / 14 cm) of Chart.

DUTCH HEEL (SEE PAGE 92)

With Green-Orange, work the heel back and forth over the 32 sts on needles 1 and 4 as follows:

Work the first and last 3 sts of each row in garter st, and the middle 26 sts in St st. Work in patt as est until 26 rows have been completed (approx 2³/₈ in / 6 cm).

TURNING THE HEEL

With Green-Orange, follow basic instructions for turning a Dutch heel, working until decreases are made with the 2 sts before and after the center 12 sts—14 sts rem in heel.

INSTEP SHAPING

Continuing with Green-Orange, return to knitting in the round, picking up and knitting 13 sts along each side of the heel flap plus 1 extra st on each side between the heel and the instep sts. Needles 2 and 3 have 16 sts each, and needles 1 and 4 now have 21 sts each—74 sts total. The end of the rnd is between needles 1 and 4.

Knit 3 rnds.

Dec rnd: Knit to last 3 sts on ndl 1, k2tog, k1; knit across needles 2 and 3; on ndl 4, k1, ssk, knit to end of rnd.

Repeat dec rnd every 3rd rnd 4 times—64 sts rem.

FOOT

Work 55 rnds in St st with Green-Orange (foot measures approx 6 in / 15.5 cm).

TOE

With Green-Orange work in St st.

Rnd 1: Knit.

Dec rnd: *Knit to last 3 sts on ndl 1, k2tog, k1, on ndl 2, k1, ssk, knit to end of needle; rep from * on needles 3 and 4.

Repeat dec rnd every other rnd 5 times, then every rnd 7 times—12 sts rem.

FINISHING

Break the yarn and run the tail through the remaining sts. Pull gently to fasten off. Weave in ends neatly on WS.

Make a second sock the same way.

Flowers and Stripes

LEVEL OF DIFFICULTY
Easy

SIZE
Teen large/women's small

MATERIALS
Yarn:

Fingering (CYCA #1)

Lana Grossa Meilenweit Fantasy (80% wool/20% nylon; 460 yd / 421 m/ 100 g), Green/Purple/Turquoise/Natural (#4848), 40 g

Lana Grossa Meilenweit 50 (80% wool/20% nylon; 230 yd / 210 m/50 g), Petrol Blue (#1338), 10 g

Regia 4-ply (75% wool/25% nylon; 229 yd / 210 m/50 g), White (#600) and Royal (#540), 10 g each

Schoeller + Stahl Fortissima (75% wool/25% nylon; 229 yd / 209 m/50 g), Violet (#1014), 10 g

Austermann Step Classic (75% wool/25% nylon; 460 yd / 421 m/100 g), Turquoise (#1018), 10 g

Needles: Set of 5 dpn U.S. size 0 (2 mm) or size needed to obtain gauge.

GAUGE
33½ sts and 43 rnds = 4 x 4 in (10 x 10 cm) in St st

30½ sts and 37 rnds = 4 x 4 in (10 x 10 cm) over Charted Pattern

Chart

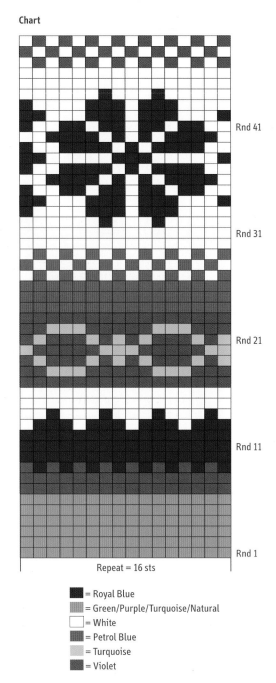

Rnd 41

Rnd 31

Rnd 21

Rnd 11

Rnd 1

Repeat = 16 sts

■ = Royal Blue
▨ = Green/Purple/Turquoise/Natural
□ = White
▨ = Petrol Blue
▨ = Turquoise
■ = Violet

PATTERN STITCHES

RIBBING
All rnds: (K2, p2) around.

STOCKINETTE STITCH (ST ST)
Working back and forth, knit RS rows, purl WS rows.
In the round, knit all rounds.

GARTER STITCH
Working back and forth, knit every row.

CHART NOTES
The charted pattern is worked in St st in the round. Each square represents one stitch and each row in the chart represents one round or row of knitting. When changing colors, strand the unused yarn loosely on the back of the work, making sure the tension remains even. To avoid long floats, twist the working yarns around each other after every 2 to 3 stitches. Chart has a repeat of 16 sts worked over 49 rnds.

INSTRUCTIONS

With Green/Purple/Turquoise/Natural, CO 64 sts. Divide sts evenly on 4 dpns and join to work in the round, being careful not to twist sts.

CUFF
Work 24 rnds (approx 2 in / 5 cm) in Ribbing.

LEG
Begin working Charted Pattern, working 4 repeats of 16 sts around. The end of the rnd is between needles 1 and 4. Work all 49 rnds of Chart (approx 5¼ in / 13.5 cm).

DUTCH HEEL (SEE PAGE 92)

With Green/Purple/Turquoise/Natural, work the heel back and forth over the 32 sts on needles 1 and 4 as follows:

Work the first and last 3 sts of each row in garter st, and the middle 26 sts in St st. Work in patt as est until 26 rows have been completed (approx 2 in / 5 cm).

TURNING THE HEEL

With Green/Purple/Turquoise/Natural, follow basic instructions for turning a Dutch heel, working until decreases are made with the 2 sts before and after the center 12 sts—14 sts rem in heel.

INSTEP SHAPING

Continuing with Green/Purple/Turquoise/Natural, return to knitting in the round, picking up and knitting 13 sts along each side of the heel flap plus 1 extra st on each side between the heel and the instep sts. Needles 2 and 3 have 16 sts each, and needles 1 and 4 now have 21 sts each—74 sts total. The end of the rnd is between needles 1 and 4.

Knit 2 rnds.

Dec rnd: Knit to last 3 sts on ndl 1, k2tog, k1; knit across needles 2 and 3; on ndl 4, k1, ssk, knit to end of rnd.

Repeat dec rnd every 3rd rnd 4 times—64 sts rem.

FOOT

With Green/Purple/Turquoise/Natural, work in St st for 56 rnds (foot measures approx 5¼ in / 13 cm).

TOE

Beginning with Turquoise, work in St st. Knit 2 rnds.

Dec rnd: *Knit to last 3 sts on ndl 1, k2tog, k1; on ndl 2, k1, ssk, knit to end of needle; rep from * on needles 3 and 4.

Repeat dec rnd every other rnd 5 times, then every rnd 7 times—12 sts rem.

FINISHING

Break the yarn and run the tail through the remaining sts. Pull gently to fasten off. Weave in ends neatly on WS.

Make a second sock the same way, making sure to start at the same place in the color sequence if you want your socks to match exactly.

Bold Effects

LEVEL OF DIFFICULTY
Intermediate

SIZE
Women's large/
men's medium

MATERIALS
Yarn:

Fingering (CYCA #1)

Regia 4-ply (75% wool/
25% nylon; 229 yd / 210
m/50 g), Black (#2066), 50 g

Regia Hand-dye Effect
(70% wool/25% nylon/
5% acrylic; 459 yd /
420 m/100g), Ruby (#6550),
30 g

Needles: Set of 5 dpn U.S.
size 0 (2 mm) or size needed
to obtain gauge.

GAUGE
32 sts and 41½ rnds =
4 x 4 in (10 x 10 cm) in St st

31 sts and 35 rnds =
4 x 4 in (10 x 10 cm) over
Charted Pattern

PATTERN STITCHES

RIBBING
All rnds: (K2, p2) around.

STOCKINETTE STITCH (ST ST)

Working back and forth, knit RS rows, purl WS rows.
In the round, knit all rounds.

Chart

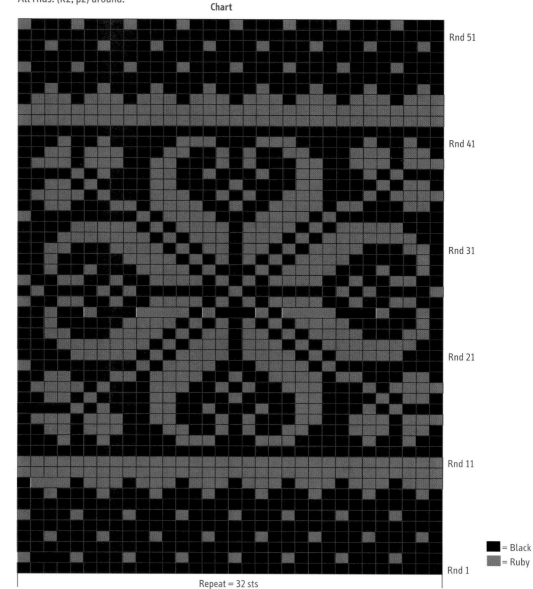

Rnd 51

Rnd 41

Rnd 31

Rnd 21

Rnd 11

Rnd 1

Repeat = 32 sts

■ = Black
▨ = Ruby

GARTER STITCH

Working back and forth, knit every row.

CHART NOTES

The charted pattern is worked in St st in the round. Each square represents one stitch and each row in the chart represents one round or row of knitting. When changing colors, strand the unused yarn loosely on the back of the work, making sure the tension remains even. To avoid long floats, twist the working yarns around each other after every 2 to 3 stitches. Chart has a repeat of 32 sts worked over 52 rnds.

INSTRUCTIONS

With Black, CO 64 sts. Divide sts evenly on 4 dpns and join to work in the round, being careful not to twist sts.

CUFF

Work 24 rnds (approx 2¼ in / 5.5 cm) in Ribbing.

LEG

Begin working Charted Pattern, working 2 repeats of 32 sts around. Arrange the stitches so the first half of a repeat is on needle 1 and the second half of a repeat is on needle 4. The end of the rnd is between needles 1 and 4. Work all 52 rnds of Chart (approx 6 in / 15 cm). Knit 3 rnds with Black.

DUTCH HEEL (SEE PAGE 92)

With Black, work the heel back and forth over the 32 sts on needles 1 and 4 as follows: Work the first and last 3 sts of each row in garter st, and the middle 26 sts in St st. Work in patt as est until 26 rows have been completed (approx 2¼ in / 5.5 cm).

TURNING THE HEEL

Follow basic instructions for turning a Dutch heel, working until decreases are made with the 2 sts before and after the center 12 sts—14 sts rem in heel.

INSTEP SHAPING

Continuing with Black, return to knitting in the round, picking up and knitting 13 sts along each side of the heel flap plus 1 extra st on each side between the heel and the instep sts. Needles 2 and 3 have 16 sts each, and needles 1 and 4 now have 21 sts each—74 sts total. The end of the rnd is between needles 1 and 4.
Knit 2 rnds.
Dec rnd: Knit to last 3 sts on ndl 1, k2tog, k1; knit across needles 2 and 3; on ndl 4, k1, ssk, knit to end of rnd.
Repeat dec rnd every 3rd rnd 4 times—64 sts rem.

FOOT

With Black, work in St st for 38 rnds (foot measures approx 3½ in / 9 cm), then work rnds 2-10 of Chart.

TOE

With Ruby, work in St st.
Rnd 1: Knit.
Dec rnd: *Knit to last 3 sts on ndl 1, k2tog, k1; on ndl 2, k1, ssk, knit to end of needle; rep from * on needles 3 and 4.
Repeat dec rnd every other rnd 5 times, then every rnd 7 times—12 sts rem.

FINISHING

Break the yarn and run the tail through the remaining sts. Pull gently to fasten off. Weave in ends neatly on WS.

Make a second sock the same way.

Geometric Shapes

Polka dots, stripes, arcs, circles, and zigzags give these socks that special je ne sais quoi. The patterns are small and easy to memorize, with a little care, you'll be knitting beautiful socks in no time.

PATTERN MIX

Instructions page 76

CIRCLES IN PURPLE, PINK & BLUE

Instructions page 78

INDIAN PATTERN
Instructions page 84

BLUE TONES
Instructions page 86

Pattern Mix

LEVEL OF DIFFICULTY
Intermediate

SIZE
Women's medium/men's small

MATERIALS
Yarn:

Fingering (CYCA #1)

Regia 4-ply Color (75% wool/
25% nylon; 229 yd / 210 m/
50 g), Blue-Gray-Graphite-
color (#6809), 30 g

Regia 4-ply (75% wool/
25% nylon; 229 yd / 210 m/
50 g), Light Gray (#1968), 30 g

Regia Hand-dye Effect (70%
wool/25% nylon/5% acrylic;
459 yd / 420 m/100 g),
Aragonite (#6557), 10 g

Regia 4-ply Trend & Color
(75% wool/25% nylon;
459 yd / 420 m/100 g), Amber
heather (#6766) and Toffee
heather (#6765), 10 g each

Austermann Step Classic
(75% wool/25% nylon;
460 yd / 421 m/100 g), Vanilla
(#1001), 10 g

Schoeller + Stahl Fortissima
Piccolino (50% wool/25%
rayon/25% nylon; 109 yd
100 m/25 g), Corn (#06), 10 g

Needles: Set of 5 dpn U.S.
size 0 (2 mm) or size needed
to obtain gauge.

GAUGE
29 sts and 39 rnds = 4 x 4 in
(10 x 10 cm) over Chart 1

30½ sts and 36½ rnds =
4 x 4 in (10 x 10 cm) over
Chart 2

PATTERN STITCHES

RIBBING
All rnds: (K2, p2) around.

STOCKINETTE STITCH (ST ST)
Working back and forth, knit RS rows, purl WS rows.
In the round, knit all rounds.

CHART NOTES
Charts 1 and 2 are worked in St st in the round. Each square
represents one stitch and each row in the chart represents
one round or row of knitting. When changing colors, strand
the unused yarn loosely on the back of the work, making
sure the tension remains even. To avoid long floats, twist
the working yarns around each other after every 2 to 3
stitches. Both Charts have a repeat of 8 sts. Chart 1 is
worked over 62 rnds and Chart 2 is worked over 55 rnds.

INSTRUCTIONS

With Light Gray, CO 64 sts. Divide sts evenly on 4 dpns and
join to work in the round, being careful not to twist sts.

CUFF
Work 24 rnds (approx 2 in / 5 cm) in Ribbing as follows:
10 rnds in Light Gray
14 rnds in Blue-Gray-Graphite-color

LEG
Begin working Chart 1, working 8 repeats of 8 sts around.
The end of the rnd is between needles 1 and 4. Work all 62
rnds (approx 6¼ in / 16 cm) of Chart 1.

SHORT-ROW HEEL
With Blue-Gray-Graphite-color, work the heel back and
forth in St st over the 32 sts on needles 1 and 4 as follows
(see basic short-row heel technique, pp 90-91):
Divide the heel stitches into 3 sections with 8 sts in the
center and 12 sts on each side. Work decreasing short-row
section, using the double-stitch technique for working
turns. When 8 sts rem in center, knit 2 rounds on all four
needles, working both loops of each double stitch
together as one stitch. End the second round at the beginning of the middle section of the heel. Work increasing
short-row section, using the double-stitch technique and
complete heel as described in the basic instructions.

FOOT
Return to working in the round following Chart 2 and picking up the double loops and knitting them together on first
rnd—64 sts. The end of the round is between needles 1
and 4.
Work all 55 rnds of Chart 2 (approx 6 in / 15 cm).

TOE
With Blue-Gray-Graphite color work in St st.
Rnd 1: Knit.
Dec rnd: *Knit to last 3 sts on ndl 1, k2tog, k1; on ndl 2, k1,
ssk, knit to end of needle; rep from * on needles 3 and 4.
Repeat dec rnd every other rnd twice, on every 4th rnd
once, then every rnd 9 times—12 sts rem.

FINISHING
Break the yarn and run the tail through the remaining sts.
Pull gently to fasten off. Weave in ends neatly on WS.

Make a second sock the same way.

Chart 1

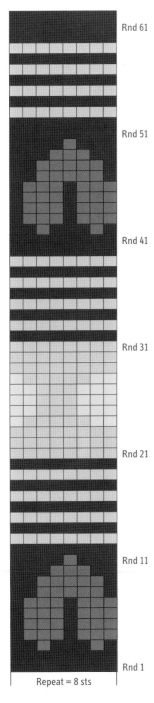

Rnd 61

Rnd 51

Rnd 41

Rnd 31

Rnd 21

Rnd 11

Rnd 1

Repeat = 8 sts

Chart 2

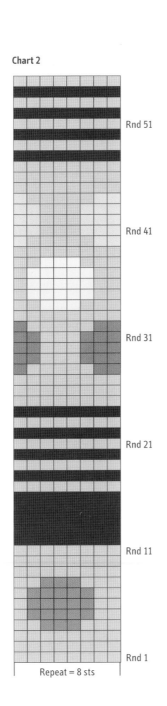

Rnd 51

Rnd 41

Rnd 31

Rnd 21

Rnd 11

Rnd 1

Repeat = 8 sts

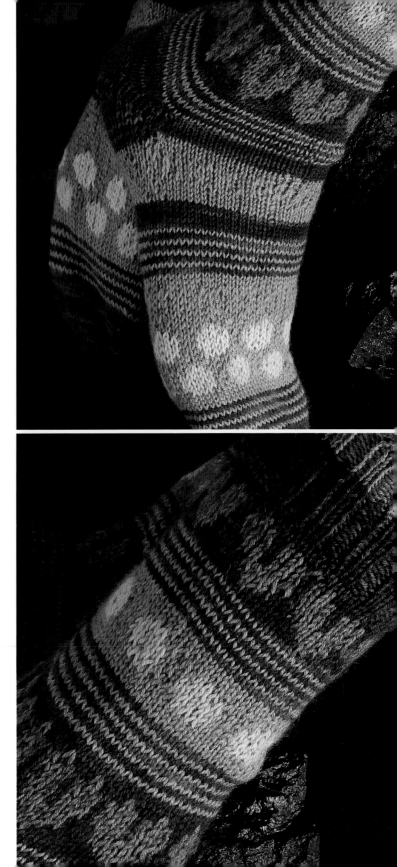

Circles in Purple, Pink & Blue

LEVEL OF DIFFICULTY
Easy

SIZE
Women's medium/men's small

MATERIALS
Yarn:

Fingering (CYCA #1)

Regia 4-ply (75% wool/ 25% nylon; 229 yd / 210 m/50 g), Light Gray Heather (#1991), 40g, Medium Gray Heather (#44) and Dove Blue (#1970), 10 g each

Regia Extra Twist Merino (75% wool/25% nylon; 229 yd / 210 m/50 g), Rose (#9351), 10 g

Lana Grossa Meilenweit 50 (80% wool/20% nylon; 230 yd / 210 m/50 g), Purple (#1336), 20 g

Needles: Set of 5 dpn U.S. size 0 (2 mm) or size needed to obtain gauge.

GAUGE
30 sts and 41½ rnds = 4 x 4 in (10 x 10 cm) over Charted Pattern

PATTERN STITCHES

RIBBING
All rnds: (K2, p2) around.

GARTER STITCH
Working back and forth, knit every row.

CHART NOTES
The charted pattern is worked in St st in the round. Each square represents one stitch and each row in the chart represents one round or row of knitting. When changing colors, strand the unused yarn loosely on the back of the work, making sure the tension remains even. To avoid long floats, twist the working yarns around each other after every 2 to 3 stitches. Chart has a repeat of 16 sts and 62 rnds.

INSTRUCTIONS

With Light Gray, CO 64 sts. Divide sts evenly on 4 dpns and join to work in the round, being careful not to twist sts.

CUFF
Work 24 rnds (approx 2 in / 5 cm) in St st. Then, work 2 rnds in garter stitch.

LEG
Begin working Chart, working 4 repeats of 16 sts around. The end of the rnd is between needles 1 and 4. Work all 62 rnds of Chart (approx 6 in / 15 cm).

DUTCH HEEL (SEE PAGE 92)
With Light Gray, work the heel back and forth over the 32 sts on needles 1 and 4 as follows:

Work the first and last 4 sts of each row in garter st, and the middle 24 sts in St st. Work in patt as est until 26 rows have been completed (approx 2¼ in / 5.5 cm).

TURNING THE HEEL
With Light Gray, follow basic instructions for turning a Dutch heel, working until decreases are made with the 2 sts before and after the center 10 sts—12 sts rem in heel.

INSTEP SHAPING
Continuing with Light Gray, return to knitting in the round, picking up and knitting 13 sts along each side of the heel flap plus 1 extra st on each side between the heel and the instep sts. Needles 2 and 3 have 16 sts each, and needles 1 and 4 now have 20 sts each—72 sts total. The end of the rnd is between needles 1 and 4.
Work in St st and stripes (2 rnds in Light Gray, 3 rnds in Medium Gray heather, and 6 rnds in Purple), then begin working Chart Pattern beginning on row 22. *At the same time*, decrease for instep as follows:
Knit 2 rnds.
Dec rnd: Knit to last 3 sts on ndl 1, k2tog, k1; knit across needles 2 and 3; on ndl 4, k1, ssk, knit to end of rnd.
Repeat dec rnd every 3rd rnd 3 times—64 sts rem.

FOOT
Work 41 rnds in Charted Pattern, ending with row 62 (approx 4 in / 10 cm).
With Light Gray, knit 2 rnds.

TOE
With Purple work in St st.
Rnd 1: Knit.
Dec rnd: *Knit to last 3 sts on ndl 1, k2tog, k1; on ndl 2, k1, ssk, knit to end of needle; rep from * on needles 3 and 4.

Chart

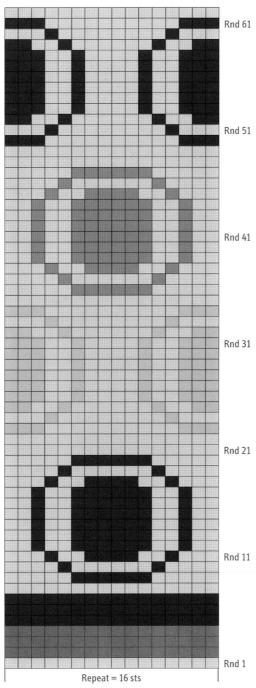

Rnd 61

Repeat dec rnd every 3rd rnd twice, then every other rnd twice, then every rnd 8 times—12 sts rem.

Rnd 51

FINISHING

Break the yarn and run the tail through the remaining sts. Pull gently to fasten off. Weave in ends neatly on WS.

Rnd 41

Make a second sock the same way.

Rnd 31

Rnd 21

Rnd 11

 = Medium Gray Heather
= Light Gray Heather
= Dove Blue
= Rose
= Purple

Rnd 1

Repeat = 16 sts

Stripes, Lozenges, and Spikes

LEVEL OF DIFFICULTY
Intermediate

SIZE
Women's medium/
men's small

MATERIALS
Yarn:

Fingering (CYCA #1)

Regia 4-ply (75% wool/
25% nylon; 229 yd / 210
m/50 g), Black (#2066), 30 g

Schoeller + Stahl Fortissima
(75% wool/25% nylon;
229 yd / 209 m/50 g),
Violet (#1014), 10 g

Austermann Royal (60%
Merino wool/20% nylon/
10% cashmere/10% silk;
219 yd / 200 m/50 g), Royal
(#25) and Taupe (#12), 10 g
each

Lana Grossa Meilenweit 50
(80% wool/20% nylon;
229 yd / 210 m/50 g), Violet
(#1336), Beige (#1301) and
Blue-gray (#1334), 10 g
each

Lana Grossa Meilenweit
Ultimo (80% wool/20%
nylon; 260 yd / 421 m/100g),
Turquoise (#2508), 20 g

Needles: Set of 5 dpn U.S.
size 1 (2.5 mm) or size
needed to obtain gauge.

GAUGE
32½ sts and 40 rnds =
4 x 4 in (10 x 10 cm) over
Chart 1

32½ sts and 40 rnds =
4 x 4 in (10 x 10 cm) over
Chart 2

PATTERN STITCHES

RIBBING

All rnds: (K2, p2) around.

STOCKINETTE STITCH (ST ST)

Working back and forth, knit RS rows, purl WS rows.
In the round, knit all rounds.

GARTER STITCH

Working back and forth, knit every row.

CHART NOTES

Charts 1 and 2 are worked in St st in the round. Each square represents one stitch and each row in the chart represents one round or row of knitting. When changing colors, strand the unused yarn loosely on the back of the work, making sure the tension remains even. Charts 1 and 2 both have repeats of 4 sts. Chart 1 is worked over 60 rnds and Chart 2 is worked over 63 rnds.

INSTRUCTIONS

With Turquoise, CO 72 sts. Divide sts evenly on 4 dpns and join to work in the round, being careful not to twist sts.

CUFF

Work 23 rnds (approx 2 in / 5 cm) in Ribbing, changing to Black after the first 3 rnds.

LEG

Begin working Chart 1 around all sts. The end of the rnd is between needles 1 and 4. Work all 36 rnds of Chart 1 (approx 6 in / 15 cm).

DUTCH HEEL (SEE PAGE 92)

With Turquoise, work the heel back and forth over the 36 sts on needles 1 and 4 as follows:
Work the first and last 4 sts of each row in garter st, and the middle 28 sts in St st. Work in patt as est until 28 rows have been completed (approx 2⅜ in / 6 cm).

TURNING THE HEEL

With Turquoise, follow basic instructions for turning a Dutch heel, working until decreases are made with the 2 sts before and after the center 10 sts—12 sts rem in heel.

INSTEP SHAPING

Continuing with Turquoise, return to knitting in the round, picking up and knitting 14 sts along each side of the heel flap plus 1 extra st on each side between the heel and the instep sts. Needles 2 and 3 have 18 sts each, and needles 1 and 4 now have 21 sts each—78 sts total. The end of the rnd is between needles 1 and 4.
Work Chart 2 and, *at the same time*, dec as follows:
Next rnd: Knit around.
Dec rnd: Knit to last 3 sts on ndl 1, k2tog, k1; knit across needles 2 and 3; on ndl 4, k1, ssk, knit to end of rnd.
Repeat dec rnd every 3rd rnd 4 times—68 sts rem.

FOOT

Work all 63 rnds of Chart 2 (approx 6¼ in / 16 cm).

TOE

With Black, work in St st.
Rnd 1: Knit.
Dec rnd: *Knit to last 3 sts on ndl 1, k2tog, k1; on ndl 2, k1, ssk, knit to end of needle; rep from * on needles 3 and 4.
Repeat dec rnd every other rnd 3 times, then every rnd 10 times—12 sts rem.

FINISHING

Break the yarn and run the
tail through the remaining
sts. Pull gently to fasten off.
Weave in ends neatly on WS.

Make a second sock the
same way.

Chart 1

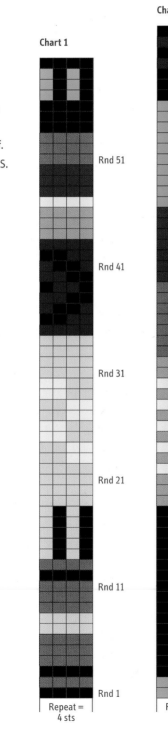

Rnd 51

Rnd 41

Rnd 31

Rnd 21

Rnd 11

Rnd 1

Repeat =
4 sts

Chart 2

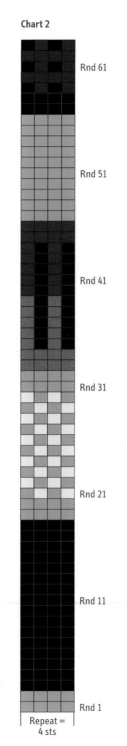

Rnd 61

Rnd 51

Rnd 41

Rnd 31

Rnd 21

Rnd 11

Rnd 1

Repeat =
4 sts

■ = Black
■ = Turquoise
■ = Violet Fortissima
■ = Blue-Gray
□ = Beige
■ = Royal Blue
■ = Violet Lana Grossa
■ = Taupe

Symphony in Blue

LEVEL OF DIFFICULTY
Intermediate

SIZE
Women's medium/
men's small

MATERIALS
Yarn:

Fingering (CYCA #1)

Lana Grossa Meilenweit 50
(80% wool/20% nylon;
229 yd / 210 m/50 g),
Eggplant (#1332), 20 g,
Turquoise # 1345), medium
Petrol Blue (# 1335) and
Lavender (#1342), 10 g each

Regia 4-ply (75% wool/
25% nylon; 229 yd / 210
m/50 g), Gray-blue mouliné
(# 616), Super White (#2080)
and Rose (#1976), 10 g each

Regia Extra Twist Merino
(75% wool/25% nylon;
229 yd / 210 m/50 g),
Petrol Blue (#9357), 10 g

Needles: Set of 5 size 1-2
U.S. (2.5 mm) double-
pointed needles

GAUGE
30½ sts and 35 rnds =
4 x 4 in (10 x 10 cm) over
Chart 1

30½ sts and 42½ rnds =
4 x 4 in (10 x 10 cm) over
Chart 2

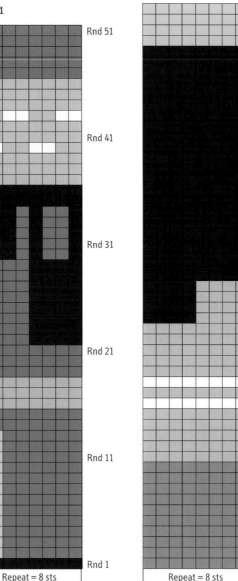

Chart 1

Rnd 51
Rnd 41
Rnd 31
Rnd 21
Rnd 11
Rnd 1

Repeat = 8 sts

Chart 2

Rnd 51
Rnd 41
3 Rnd 1
Rnd 21
Rnd 11
Rnd 1

Repeat = 8 sts

PATTERN STITCHES

RIBBING
All rnds: (K2, p2) around.

STOCKINETTE STITCH (ST ST)
Working back and forth, knit RS rows, purl WS
rows.
In the round, knit all rounds.

GARTER STITCH
Working back and forth, knit every row.

CHART NOTES
Charts 1 and 2 are worked in St st in the round.
Each square represents one stitch and each row
in the chart represents one round or row of
knitting. When changing colors, strand the
unused yarn loosely on the back of the work,
making sure the tension remains even. To avoid
long floats, twist the working yarns around
each other after every 2 to 3 stitches. Both
charts have repeats of 8 sts. Chart 1 is worked
over 51 rnds and Chart 2 is worked over 53 rnds.

INSTRUCTIONS

With Eggplant, CO 64 sts. Divide sts evenly on 4
dpns and join to work in the round, being careful not to twist sts.

= Eggplant
= Petrol Blue
= Turquoise
= Medium Petrol Blue
= Super White
= Lavender
= Rose
= Gray-Blue Mouliné

CUFF

Work 24 rnds (approx 2 in / 5 cm) in Ribbing.

LEG

Begin working Chart 1. The end of the rnd is between needles 1 and 4. Work all 46 rnds of Chart 1 (approx 5 in / 13 cm), then work sts on needles 1 in Petrol Blue and sts on needles 3 and 4 in Gray-blue mouliné, twisting colors after every 2 or 3 sts as described in Basic Techniques (page 94). Work even until leg measures 5¾ in / 14.5 cm from ribbing (51 rnds complete on leg).

DUTCH HEEL (SEE PAGE 92)

With colors as established, work the heel back and forth over the 32 sts on needles 1 and 4 using the intarsia technique (pick up new color from below old color to cross strands and prevent holes) as follows:

Work the first and last 4 sts of each row in garter st, and the middle 24 sts in St st. Work patts as est until 28 rows have been completed (approx 2¼ in / 5.5 cm).

TURNING THE HEEL

With Gray-blue mouliné, follow the basic instructions for turning a Dutch heel, working until decreases are made with the 2 sts before and after the center 10 sts—12 sts rem in heel.

INSTEP SHAPING

Continuing with Gray-blue mouliné, return to knitting in the round, picking up and knitting 13 sts along each side of the heel flap plus 1 extra st on each side between the heel and the instep sts. Needles 2 and 3 have 16 sts each, and needles 1 and 4 now have 20 sts each—72 sts total. The end of the rnd is between needles 1 and 4. Work Chart 2 and, *at the same time*, dec as follows:

Next rnd: Knit around.

Dec rnd: Knit to last 3 sts on ndl 1, k2tog, k1; knit across needles 2 and 3; on ndl 4, k1, ssk, knit to end of rnd.

Repeat dec rnd every 3rd rnd twice, then every other round once—64 sts rem.

FOOT

Work all 53 rnds of Chart 2 (approx 5 in / 12.5 cm).

TOE

With Petrol Blue, work in St st.

Knit 4 rnds.

Dec rnd: *Knit to last 3 sts on ndl 1, k2tog, k1; on ndl 2, k1, ssk, knit to end of needle; rep from * on needles 3 and 4.

Repeat dec rnd every 3rd rnd twice, then every other rnd once, then every rnd 10 times—8 sts rem.

FINISHING

Break the yarn and run the tail through the remaining sts. Pull gently to fasten off. Weave in ends neatly on WS.

Make a second sock the same way.

Indian Pattern

LEVEL OF DIFFICULTY
Intermediate

SIZE
Women's medium/
men's small

MATERIALS
Yarn:

Fingering (CYCA #1)

Regia 4-ply (75% wool/
25% nylon; 229 yd / 210
m/50 g), Black (#2066) and
Ice Blue (#2018), 30 g each

Lana Grossa Meilenweit
(80% wool/20% nylon;
230 yd / 210 m/50 g),
Mint-gray (#1334), 30 g

Needles: Set of 5 dpn U.S.
size 0 (2 mm) or size needed
to obtain gauge.

GAUGE
30½ sts and 37½ rnds =
4 x 4 in (10 x 10 cm) over
Chart 1

32 sts and 39 rnds =
4 x 4 in (10 x 10 cm) over
Chart 2

Chart 1

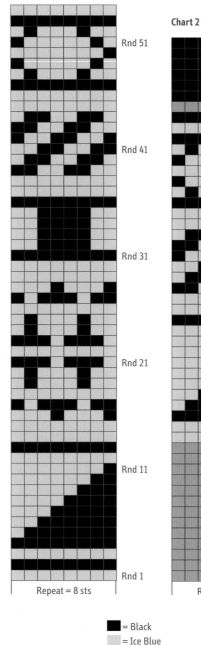

Rnd 51

Rnd 41

Rnd 31

Rnd 21

Rnd 11

Rnd 1

Repeat = 8 sts

Chart 2

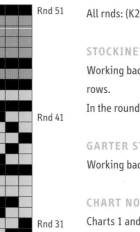

Rnd 51

Rnd 41

Rnd 31

Rnd 21

Rnd 11

Rnd 1

Repeat = 8 sts

■ = Black
▨ = Ice Blue
▨ = Mint-Gray

PATTERN STITCHES

RIBBING
All rnds: (K2, p2) around.

STOCKINETTE STITCH (ST ST)
Working back and forth, knit RS rows, purl WS
rows.
In the round, knit all rounds.

GARTER STITCH
Working back and forth, knit every row.

CHART NOTES
Charts 1 and 2 are worked in St st in the round.
Each square represents one stitch and each row in
the chart represents one round or row of knitting.
When changing colors, strand the unused yarn
loosely on the back of the work, making sure the
tension remains even. To avoid long floats, twist
the working yarns around each other after every 2
to 3 stitches. Both charts have repeats of 8 sts.
Chart 1 is worked over 54 rnds and Chart 2 is
worked over 51 rnds.

INSTRUCTIONS

With Mint-gray, CO 64 sts. Divide sts evenly on 4
dpns and join to work in the round, being careful
not to twist sts.

CUFF
Work 24 rnds (approx 2¼ in / 5.5 cm) in Ribbing,
changing to Ice Blue after rnd 12.

LEG

Begin working Chart 1. The end of the rnd is between needles 1 and 4. Work all 54 rnds of Chart 1 (approx 5¾ in / 14.5 cm).

DUTCH HEEL (SEE PAGE 92)

With Mint-gray, work the heel back and forth over the 32 sts on needles 1 and 4 as follows: Work the first and last 4 sts of each row in garter st, and the middle 24 sts in St st. Work in patt as est until 28 rows have been completed (approx 2¼ in /5.5 cm).

TURNING THE HEEL

With Mint-gray, follow basic instructions for turning a Dutch heel, working until decreases are made with the 2 sts before and after the center 10 sts—12 sts rem in heel.

INSTEP SHAPING

Continuing with Mint-gray, return to knitting in the round, picking up and knitting 13 sts along each side of the heel flap plus 1 extra st on each side between the heel and the instep sts. Needles 2 and 3 have 16 sts each, and needles 1 and 4 now have 20 sts each—72 sts total. The end of the rnd is between needles 1 and 4.
Knit 2 rnds.
Dec rnd: Knit to last 3 sts on ndl 1, k2tog, k1; knit across needles 2 and 3; on ndl 4, k1, ssk, knit to end of rnd.
Repeat dec rnd every 3rd rnd 3 times—64 sts rem.

FOOT

Work all 51 rnds of Chart 2 (approx 5 in / 13 cm).

TOE

With Mint-gray work in St st.
Knit 3 rnds.
Dec rnd: *Knit to last 3 sts on ndl 1, k2tog, k1; on ndl 2, k1, ssk, knit to end of needle; rep from * on needles 3 and 4.
Repeat dec rnd every 3rd rnd twice, then every other rnd twice, then every rnd 8 times—12 sts rem.

FINISHING

Break the yarn and run the tail through the remaining sts. Pull gently to fasten off. Weave in ends neatly on WS.

Make a second sock the same way.

Blue Tones

SIZE
Women's medium/
men's small

MATERIALS
Yarn:

Fingering (CYCA #1)

Regia 4-ply (75% wool/
25% nylon; 229 yd / 210
m/50 g), Royal (#540), 35 g,
Cardinal (#1078), Lemon
(#2019) and Lavender
(#1988), 20 g each

Regia Extra Twist Merino
(75% wool/25% nylon;
229 yd / 210 m/50 g),
Light Blue (#9355), 20 g

Needles: Set of 5 dpn U.S.
size 0 (2 mm) or size needed
to obtain gauge.

GAUGE
29 sts and 37½ rnds =
4 x 4 in (10 x 10 cm) over
Chart 1

32 sts and 37½ rnds =
4 x 4 in (10 x 10 cm) over
Chart 2

PATTERN STITCHES

RIBBING
All rnds: (K2, p2) around.

STOCKINETTE STITCH (ST ST)
Working back and forth, knit RS rows, purl WS rows.
In the round, knit all rounds.

GARTER STITCH
Working back and forth, knit every row.

CHART NOTES
Charts 1 and 2 are worked in St st in the round. Each square
represents one stitch and each row in the chart represents
one round or row of knitting. When changing colors, strand
the unused yarn loosely on the back of the work, making
sure the tension remains even. To avoid long floats, twist
the working yarns around each other after every 2 to 3
stitches.

On Chart 1, rows 1-22 and 44-58 have a multiple of 8 sts and
the motif on rows 23-43 has a repeat of 32 sts. Chart 2 has a
repeat of 4 sts and is worked over 60 rnds.

INSTRUCTIONS

With Royal and U.S. size 0 (2 mm) needles, CO 64 sts. Divide
sts evenly on 4 dpns and join to work in the round, being
careful not to twist sts.

CUFF
Work 24 rnds (approx 2¼ in / 5.5 cm) in Ribbing.

LEG
Begin working Chart 1. The end of the rnd is between needles 1 and 4. Work all 58 rnds of Chart 1 (approx 6¼ in /
15.5 cm).

DUTCH HEEL (SEE PAGE 92)
With Royal, work the heel back and forth over the 32 sts on
needles 1 and 4 as follows:
Work the first and last 3 sts of each row in garter st, and the
middle 26 sts in St st. Work in patt as est until 26 rows have
been completed (approx 2¼ in / 5.5 cm).

TURNING THE HEEL
With Royal, follow basic instructions for turning a Dutch
heel, working until decreases are made with the 2 sts
before and after the center 12 sts—14 sts rem in heel.

INSTEP SHAPING
With Light Blue, return to knitting in the round, picking up

and knitting 13 sts along each side of the heel flap plus 1 extra st on each side between the heel and the instep sts. Needles 2 and 3 have 16 sts each, and needles 1 and 4 now have 21 sts each—74 sts total. The end of the rnd is between needles 1 and 4.

Begin working Chart 2 and, *at the same time*, dec as follows:

Note To maintain pattern as decreases are worked, in rnd 3 of Chart 2, at the end of needle 1 and at the beginning of the needle 4, work 4 sts of Light Blue between Royal Blue sts.

Next rnd: Knit.

Dec rnd: Knit to last 3 sts on ndl 1, k2tog, k1; knit across needles 2 and 3; on ndl 4, k1, ssk, knit to end of rnd.

Repeat dec rnd every 3rd rnd 4 times—64 sts rem.

FOOT

Work all 60 rnds of Chart 2 (approx 6¼ in / 16 cm).

TOE

With Royal, work in St st. Knit 2 rnds.

Dec rnd: *Knit to last 3 sts on ndl 1, k2tog, k1; on ndl 2, k1, ssk, knit to end of needle; rep from * on needles 3 and 4.

Repeat dec rnd every other rnd 5 times, then every rnd 7 times—12 sts rem.

FINISHING

Break the yarn and run the tail through the remaining sts. Pull gently to fasten off. Weave in ends neatly on WS.

Make a second sock the same way.

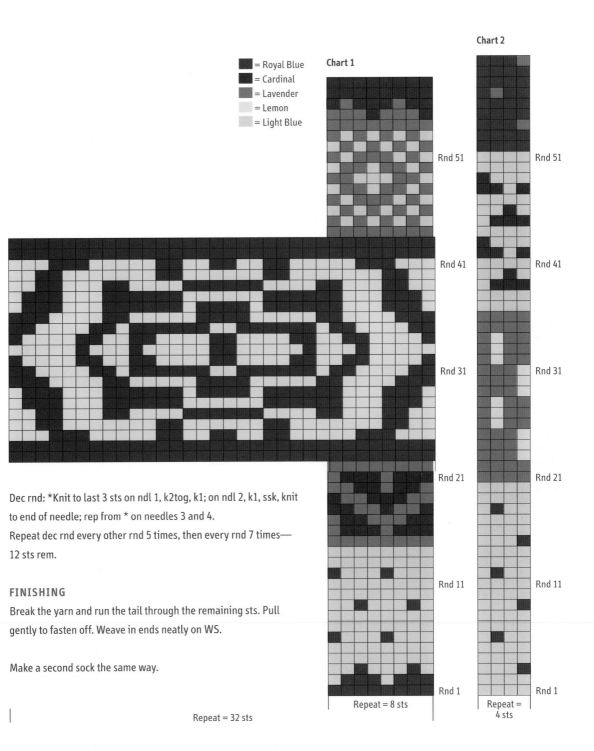

= Royal Blue
= Cardinal
= Lavender
= Lemon
= Light Blue

Chart 1

Chart 2

Rnd 51

Rnd 41

Rnd 31

Rnd 21

Rnd 11

Rnd 1

Repeat = 8 sts

Repeat = 32 sts

Repeat = 4 sts

Basic Techniques

Hand knitted socks are now more popular than ever. The beautiful sock yarns available and the soothing process of knitting both contribute to this continued popularity. Basic techniques such as knitting cuffs, heels, and toes are explained in detail in the following sections. A lesson on two-color stranded knitting is also included for beginners in knitting with multiple colors or for those who need a refresher.

ANATOMY OF A SOCK

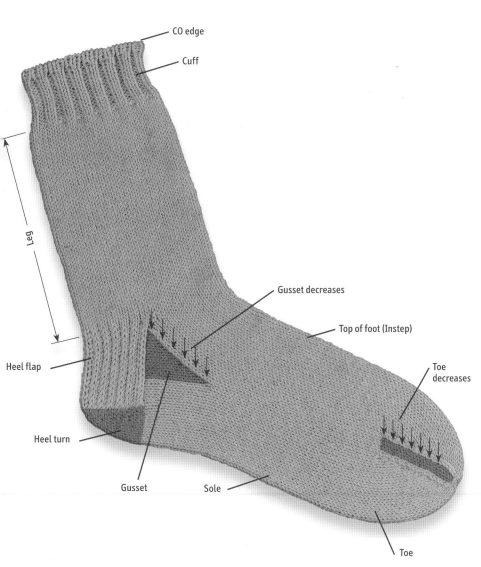

CO edge

Cuff

Leg

Gusset decreases

Top of foot (Instep)

Heel flap

Toe decreases

Heel turn

Gusset

Sole

Toe

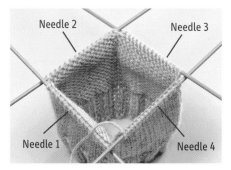

Needle 2

Needle 3

Needle 1

Needle 4

Needles are numbered starting from the yarn tail and clockwise in the direction of knitting.

CASTING ON

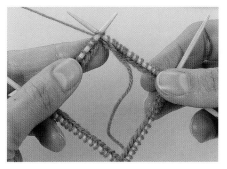

After casting on, divide the stitches equally onto four double-pointed needles. A fifth needle will be used for knitting. Make sure the stitches are not twisted and the cast-on edge is facing in the same direction on all of the needles. To begin knitting, *work across the stitches on the needle in your left hand using an empty needle. Rotate the work and repeat from * three times. Needle 1 is the beginning of the round and needle 4 is the end of the round. The yarn tail marks the end of the round, so no stitch marker is needed.

LEG

The sock leg is worked in the round, beginning with the cuff. Cuffs are most often worked in ribbing (for example k1, p1 or k2, p2), because ribbing is much more elastic than stockinette stitch and other pattern stitches. You can work the leg in ribbing, stockinette stitch, or another decorative pattern stitch. After the heel is worked, the foot is also worked in the round.

SHORT-ROW HEEL

A short-row heel is worked back-and-forth on the stitches on needles 1 and 4. Because the short-row heel is not as long as a heel with a flap and a heel turn (see Dutch heel page 92), to lengthen the heel you may want to work Stockinette stitch on the back of the leg for about ¼-½ in (1-2 cm), while continuing the pattern on the front of the leg. If necessary, you can rearrange the stitches on the needles to fit the pattern on the front of the leg. Before beginning the heel, make sure you have put the stitches back in the original position, so the heel can be worked on half of the total number of stitches in the sock.

Divide the heel into three equal sections (or as indicated in the pattern). The heel is worked in short-rows with double-stitches created after each turn. Work a double-stitch as follows: Wyif, slip the next stitch purlwise, then bring the working yarn to the front and pull it taut, up and over the top of the left needle to the back so that the two strands of yarn from the stitch below are pulled up forming two loops. To prevent holes, make sure the double-stitch is not too loose.

Part 1
In the first section of the heel, each row is worked with 1 less stitch than the previous row, until only the stitches in the center third are worked.

Row 1 (RS): Knit across all heel stitches, turn.

Row 2 (WS): Work a double-stitch, bring the yarn to the front between the needles, purl to the end of the row, turn.

Row 3: Work a double stitch, knit to the first double-stitch, turn.

Row 4: Work a double stitch, yarn to front, purl to the first double-stitch, turn.

Repeat rows 3 and 4 until all of the stitches in the first and third sections have been worked as double-stitches. The last double-stitch is knitted on a RS row.

Knit 2 rounds on all four needles, working both loops of each double stitch together as one stitch. End the second round at the beginning of the middle section of the heel.

Part 2

In the second section of the heel, each row is worked with 1 more stitch than the previous row, until all of the heel stitches have been worked.

Row 1 (RS): Knit across the middle section of the heel, turn.

Row 2 (WS): Work a double-stitch, yarn to front, purl across the rest of the sts in the middle section.

Row 3: Work a double-stitch, knit up to the first double stitch, knit the double stitch, knit the next stitch, turn.

Row 4: Work a double-stitch, yarn to front, purl up to the first double-stitch, purl the double stitch, purl the next stitch, turn.

Repeat rows 3 and 4 until all of the stitches in the first and third sections are double-stitches. Return to knitting in the round, working both legs of each double-stitch together as 1 stitch in the first round.

Note: There is no gusset shaping with a short-row heel.

The classic heel for hand-knit socks is also called a Dutch heel. It is made with a heel flap and a heel turn, followed by gusset shaping on the instep.

The flap is worked back and forth on the stitches on needles 1 and 4. Slip the first stitch of every row purlwise wyib for a selvedge that will make it easier to pick up stitches on the sides of the flap after the heel is complete. To emphasize the heel shaping, the first 3 or 4 stitches of the row can be worked in garter stitch with the remaining stitches in the center worked in stockinette stitch.

When the flap is the required length, divide the stitches into three equal sections for turning the heel. If the number of stitches in the heel is not divisible by three, put the extra stitches in the middle section. Work the heel turn back and forth over the middle section as follows:

Row 1 (RS): Knit to the last stitch in the center section, ssk (working the last center stitch together with the first stitch in the side section). Turn.

Row 2 (WS): Slip 1, purl to the last st in the center section, p2tog (working the last center stitch together with the first stitch in the side section). Turn.

Row 3: Slip 1, knit to the last stitch in the center section, ssk (working the last stitch together with the first stitch in the side section). Turn. Repeat rows 2 and 3 until only the stitches of the center section remain. End after working a WS row.

Return to working in the round as follows: With needle 1, knit across the heel stitches and then pick up and knit 1 stitch in each slipped stitch along the side of the heel flap. Work across the stitches on needles 2 and 3, keeping the stitches divided in equal sections. With needle 4, pick up and knit 1 stitch in each slipped stitch along the side of the heel flap, then knit across half of the original heel stitches. Needles 1 and 4 should each have the same number of stitches. The end of the round falls between needles 1 and 4, in the center of the heel.

BAND TOE

For a band toe, the top of the toe is worked on needles 2 and 3, and the bottom of the toe on needles 1 and 4; decreases are made on the sides of the foot.

*On needle 1, knit to the last 3 sts, k2tog, k1. On needle 2, k1, sl 1-k1-psso, knit to the end of the needle. Repeat from * on needles 3 and 4.

The decreases are repeated every other round, or as indicated in the pattern, until 3 or 4 stitches remain on each needle. To close the toe, thread the tail of the yarn on a tapestry needle and draw it through all of the remaining stitches twice. Pull gently to gather the toe, put the yarn tail to the inside of the sock and weave in the end.

STAR TOE

For a star toe, decreases are spread evenly around. To work a star toe, you must have an even number of stitches on each needle (dividing the total number of stitches in the sock into 8 equal sections).

Note If you have an odd number of stitches per needle, in the first round, k2tog at the beginning of each needle. Then start the decreases for the star shaping in the next round.

*Knit to the last 2 sts in the section, k2tog. Repeat from * around.
The number of stitches between decreases is the number of rounds to work even before the next decrease round.

For example: If your sock has 64 sts, divided into 16 sts on each needle, then each section of the toe will be 8 stitches (8x2=16).
First decrease rnd: (K6, k2tog) around.
Knit 6 rnds even.
Second decrease rnd: (K5, k2tog) around.
Knit 5 rnds even.
Continue in this fashion—with 1 less stitch before each decrease and 1 less row before each decrease round— until 1 stitch remains on each needle.
To close the toe, thread the tail of the yarn on a tapestry needle and draw it through all of the remaining stitches twice. Pull gently to gather the toe, put the yarn tail to the inside of the sock and weave in the end.

Note A star toe can also be worked in Rev St st, with all stitches purled, and the decreases worked as p2tog.

TWO-COLOR STRANDED KNITTING

Two-color stranded knitting, sometimes called Jacquard or Fair Isle color work, is worked with 2 or more colors per row or round, with one color as the main background color and one or more contrasting colors for the pattern. Stranded color patterns are usually worked in stockinette stitch in the round with the unused color stranded loosely across the back of the work. The more stitches knitted in one color, the longer the floats of un-knitted yarn will be. Floats should never be more than 8 or 10 stitches long when working with sock yarn on U.S. sizes 0-2 (2-3 mm) needles.

WEAVING IN FLOATS

If you have long floats in your knitting, there is a chance that you will catch and pull these. To avoid this, weave the unused yarn in behind the working yarn about halfway through the span of stitches. When you weave the unused color in this fashion, sometimes it shows through the pattern when the fabric is stretched. Don't weave in the unused color in the same spot on every row, or the contrasting color may create a visible stripe on the right side of the fabric.

YARD TENSION

To achieve a smooth surface on your knitting, it is important to strand the unused color across the back of the work with an even tension. To avoid puckers in the fabric when changing colors, pull the stitches on the right needle apart to match the distance between stitches in the knitted fabric. Hold these stitches in place with the index finger of your right hand, so, when you knit the next stitches with the other color, they will maintain the proper gauge.

CHANGING NEEDLES

When changing needles, it is also best to pull the stitches on the right needle apart and also hold the unused color close to the back of the work so it does not stretch diagonally across the corner between needles, forming a pucker at the join. After knitting the first stitch in the new color, adjust the needles into a more comfortable position.

Note Beginners may find it easier to work with two circular needles so there will only be two joins to worry about instead of four.

HOLDING THE YARNS

The way you carry your yarns when working with two or more colors at the same time depends on individual preference and takes practice. Comfort and smooth tension are more important than speed. To find the style of knitting that works best for you, try several techniques and see which is most comfortable.

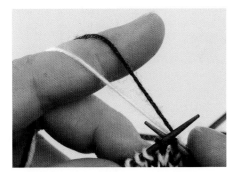

CARRYING BOTH COLORS IN YOUR LEFT HAND

Many continental knitters carry both colors over their left index finger, with both yarns tensioned around their little finger. If one color is used more often than the other, the working yarn will be used up faster and will quickly tighten around your little finger.

Carrying both colors in one hand allows you to quickly adjust the movement of the yarn because both are always in position to make the next stitch. One disadvantage to this technique is that you may always make your stitches using the yarn that is closest to the needle, twisting the strands together. This will most likely not be visible on the finished garment, but it can form lumps in the knitting.

To reduce the tendency to twist the strands, drape the first yarn from back to front over your index finger and drape the second color from front to back. Now tension both strands by wrapping

them around your little finger. This helps stop the threads from twisting extensively. However, it is difficult to keep both strands moving at the same speed.

Note For English/American style knitters, both yarns can also be carried in the right hand, with the needed color being thrown to create each stitch.

CARRYING ONE COLOR IN EACH HAND

Another popular technique is carrying one yarn in each hand, using both the right and left index finger. Sometimes this creates a problem if each hand has a different tension, but it is possible to learn to knit evenly so both colors have the same tension. This technique takes some practice and is suitable for advanced knitters.

WORKING WITH ONE COLOR AT A TIME

You can also knit with two colors, carrying your yarn in your normal way over your index finger. To change colors, simply drop the color you are finished with, and pick up the needed color to work the next stitch, remembering to keep the floats of the unused color loose on the back of the work.

Maintaining an even tension with both colors is easiest in this technique. Even beginners can achieve good results quickly. This technique also makes it very easy to twist the yarns in the middle of long floats, because you can easily see when and if the strands have been crossed.

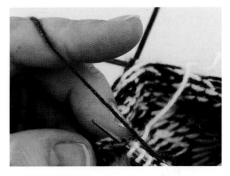

GAUGE SWATCH

Stitches in two-color stranded knitting are usually narrower than stitches in plain stockinette stitch, so more stitches are required to knit a sock of the same size. Stranded color patterns are also slightly less elastic. However, the floats running inside, make these socks thicker and warmer than single-color socks made from the same yarn.

Washing and blocking the socks flat or on sock blockers will even out any irregularities in the tension.

SIZES FOR 4-PLY SOCK YARN

TOTAL STITCHES / STITCHES PER NEEDLE	22/23 Toddler 12-24 months	24/25 Toddler 2 yrs	26/27 Toddler 3 yrs	28/29 Toddler 4 yrs	30/31 Child 6 yrs	32/33 Child's 8/10 yrs teen small	34/35 Teen medium/ women's x-small	36/37 Teen large/ women's small	38/39 Women's medium/ men's small	40/41 Women's large/ men's medium	42/43 Women's x-large/ men's large	44/45 Men's x-large	46/47 Men's 2x
Stitches per needle	44/11	48/12	48/12	52/13	52/13	56/14	56/14	60/15	60/15	64/16	64/16	68/17	72/18
Stitches in heel	22	24	24	26	26	28	28	30	30	32	32	34	36
Rows in heel flap	22	24	24	26	26	28	28	30	30	32	32	34	36
Sts in sections for short-row heel and Classic heel turn	7/8/7	8/8/8	8/8/8	8/10/8	8/10/8	9/10/9	9/10/9	10/10/10	10/10/10	10/12/10	10/12/10	11/12/11	12/12/12
Stitches rem in heel after heel turn	11	12	12	13	13	14	14	15	15	16	16	17	17
Foot length to beginning of toe—inch (cm)	4½ (11.5)	5 (12.5)	5½ (14)	5½ (14)	6¼ (15.5)	6¾ (17)	7 (18)	7¼ (18.5)	8 (20)	8¼ (21)	8¾ (22)	9 (22.5)	9½ (24)
Spacing of decrease rounds on toe after first decrease in 4th round													
Every 3rd round (X times)	1x	1x	1x	2x	2x	2x	2x	2x	2x	2x	2x	2x	2x
Every other round (X times)	2x	3x	3x	3x	3x	3x	3x	3x	3x	3x	3x	4x	4x
Every round (X times)	4x	5x	5x	5x	5x	6x	6x	6x	6x	7x	7x	7x	8x
Total foot length—inch (cm)	5¾ (14.5)	6¼ (15.5)	6¾ (17)	7 (18)	7¾ (19.5)	8¼ (21)	8¾ (22)	9¼ (23.5)	9¾ (25)	10½ (26.5)	10¾ (27.5)	11 (28.5)	11¾ (30)

ABBREVIATIONS

beg	begin, beginning
cm	centimeter(s)
CO	cast on
dpn(s)	double-pointed needle(s)
est	established
g	gram(s)
in	inch(es)
k	knit
k2tog	knit two together
m	meter(s)
ndl(s)	needle(s)
p	purl
p2tog	purl two together
patt(s)	pattern(s)
rem	remain, remaining
rev	reverse
rep	repeat
rnd(s)	round(s)
RS	right side
sl	slip
ssk	slip 1 knitwise, slip 1 knitwise; insert left needle into loops and k2tog
St st	Stockinette stitch
st(s)	stitch(es)
WS	wrong side
wyib	with yarn in back
wyif	with yarn in front
yd(s)	yard(s)

YARN INFORMATION

For more information on selecting or substituting yarn contact your local yarn shop or an online store, they are familiar with all types of yarns and would be happy to help you. Yarns come and go so quickly and there are so many beautiful sock yarns available.